THE MEMOIRS OF
CHIEF RED FOX

The Memoirs

OF

CHIEF RED FOX

With an Introduction
by Cash Asher

McGRAW-HILL BOOK COMPANY
New York St. Louis San Francisco Düsseldorf
London Mexico Panama Sydney Toronto

LIBRARY OF CONGRESS CATALOG CARD NUMBER: 70-146473

THIRD PRINTING

07-051362-7

Contents

[v]

Introduction

by Cash Asher

CHIEF RED FOX, as this, his book, goes to press, prevails among the Sioux Indians as a statuesque, historical figure, an advocate of their ancestral rights and a recorder of their place among the races of man. Born on June 11, 1870, in the foothills of the Big Horn Mountains, he heard the firing of the guns when the Indian warriors, under the command of his uncle, Crazy Horse, defeated Custer's cavalry. Here is the recital of his long and interesting life as a lone Red Man drifting across the prairies of White civilization and exchanging greetings with kings, scientists, writers, and artists who were flexing their intellectual and physical muscles in the cultural centers of the world.

Buffalo Bill, Thomas Edison, Alexander Graham Bell, the King of England, the Kaiser of Germany, Jack London, Will Rogers, and "Teddy" Roosevelt were among the dignitaries and celebrities who came into the tepee that symbolized his origins and to which he clung because it represented the unspoiled wilderness he remembered from the cradle days of America.

One critic, reading the manuscript, described it as a dramatic and sensitive document depicting the events, conflicts, and personalities of an unparalleled century in mankind's efforts to understand the creation and conquer space.

I first became interested in Chief Red Fox through his son, William Woodrow Red Fox, who attended my class in creative writing at Del Mar College in Corpus Christi, Texas. The Chief, then ninety-eight years old, had filled fourteen "Big Chief" school tablets with notes about the Indians, comments on their relations with the White man, and biographical information about his own life. Naturally, his son was interested when I told him of my connection with The American Indian Defense Association, and asked me if I would read and evaluate the notes the Chief had written, with a view to having them published. I was intrigued, of course, by the invitation.

The penciled writing in his memory books was legible, factually accurate, and at times eloquent. He had recorded information and impressions of the people who inhabited America when Christopher Columbus discovered it in 1492. He was born 378 years after that date, and had lived through nearly another century, during which time almost everything he knew as a boy had collapsed under the feet of conquerors.

To the distressed, persecuted, and adventurous inhabitants of Europe, who had fled from their homelands, crossed the Atlantic in sailing ships, and settled in this remote wilderness between two oceans, the Indians were no more important than the grizzly bear, the mountain lion, the plains-roaming buffalo, or the immense flocks of ducks, geese, pelicans, eagles, and other birds that decorated the skies. The rivers of this new world were clear and unpolluted, and many varieties of fish darted over the rapids, or spawned and rested in deep pools. The marshlands produced bounteous harvests of wild berries, plums, crabapples, and other fruits. Deer, elk, moose, quail, partridge, and many other species of edible game abounded in the mountains, on the prairies, and along the banks of streams and lakes in this enchanted wilderness.

The Indians never destroyed, nor did they kill anything except when it was needed for food. Nature prevailed and flourished for untold centuries, unchanged by the Indian. It had given him meats, nuts, vegetables to eat, leather and feathers for his clothing, poles for his tepees, bones for his dishes, the ribs of field mice for his fishhooks, hemp for his rope, and skins for his canoes.

Several weeks were required for me to read and evaluate the information written in the tablets before committing my time to the task of readying it for publication. After I agreed to this undertaking, I employed a stenographer to type this writing from the notebooks, which filled sixty-two double-spaced pages. With this mass of history before me, I organized it into chapters, and after the elimination of unimportant details, supplying others, and verifying dates and accounts through a file of data from the Smithsonian Institution, I used whatever talent I possessed to bring the text into focus under the harsh lights of the twentieth century.

Many vivid etchings came through the notebooks, along with lamentations from the soul of the man who wrote in them. There are no better words I can bring together to describe what had happened than to say that Chief Red Fox had seen the citadels of civilization overwhelm the primitive campsite of man, who was born under the stars in a wilderness paradise of creation.

I first met the Chief in the early part of December, 1969, when he came to Corpus Christi for his annual month's vacation. I will always consider this meeting one of the outstanding privileges of my life. As a newspaper reporter I have interviewed many personalities who gave glamor to the twentieth century, including Clarence Darrow, Helen Keller, Billy Sunday, Will Rogers, and Evelyn Walsh McLean, but none fascinated me more than this patriarch whose mind was like a golden file cabinet crammed with wisdom, conditioned by philosophy, guided by perception and inspired by interpretation. I was neither surprised nor disillusioned when I looked into his face, for he measured up to the linguistic artifacts he had assembled. His handshake was warm and strong. He seemed to comprehend me with instant intuition, and put his arm across my shoulder, admitting me into the personal universe where he dwells.

We got along famously, and symbolically smoked a peace pipe before the fireside of his son's home as we discussed his life on the American frontier, turned the pages of his notebooks, and opened the floodgates of his memory. He smoked three cigars during the first of our meetings and informed me, as I emptied the ash tray, that his average daily consumption of the black stogies was eighteen.

"The tobacco plant is full of vitamins," he told me, and added with a twinkle in his eyes, "a most pleasant way to get them."

I found him entirely engrossing and almost unbelievable, for he identified with a past that I knew only through history, and a future that intrigued him more than it did many teen-agers who were intent on tearing the world apart.

Working from the information obtained in our informal talks and the notebooks, I faithfully tried to keep his character in focus as that of an individual who has emerged from primitive America and learned how to conform with the customs, practices, and demands of the White man's civilization.

We have to admire this man who enters the

second hundred years of his life with visions in his mind, his eyes sparkling with anticipation for the future, his thoughts sustained by imagination. Chief Red Fox has admirably adapted to the format and formulas of his conquerors; his life has been picturesque and rewarding, yet as he stands on the threshold of time with hands outstretched toward his lost heritage there is a cry on his lips: "How empty is my wilderness!"

THE MEMOIRS OF
CHIEF RED FOX

CHAPTER I

HOW EMPTY IS
MY WILDERNESS

ALMOST everything I knew as a child has passed away, leaving the world empty of the arts and culture of the Red man who lived on the plains, deserts, and mountains before the White man came. The blood of 20,000,000 buffalo has been spilled into the Western plains. The wild horse has been enslaved behind the plow; the vast primeval forest cut down; the eagle shot from the sky; the clear rivers, streams, and lakes have been polluted and the atmosphere changed into a poison covering for a ball of mud contaminating space. And the Indian who once blended into the poetic wilderness is a prisoner of the civilization that overwhelmed him. The changes of a single century have refashioned him into a muddy-complexioned White man, stuttering and stammering through avenues of despair.

I could continue with this jeremiad, but my own life intrudes to still my words. Mentally and physically I have found enjoyment, but spiritually I have been a mourner at the bedside of a dying race. I have achieved peace by accepting the inevitable destiny for the people whose blood runs through my veins and whose sublime love of nature has always been in my mind.

I have acted in the movies and in Wild West shows, and served as an interpreter between the Indian and the White man in many conferences. I have met presidents and kings, writers, scientists, and artists. I have had much joy and received many honors, but I have never forgotten my wild, free childhood when I lived in a tepee and heard the calling of the coyotes under the stars ... when the night winds, the sun, and everything else in our primitive world reflected the wisdom and benevolence of the Great Spirit. I remember seeing my mother bending over an open fire toasting buffalo meat, and my father returning at night with an antelope on his shoulder. I remember playing with the other children on the banks of a clean river, and I shall never forget when my grandfather taught me how to make a bow and arrow from hard wood and flint, and a fishhook from the rib of a field mouse. I am not sentimental, but memories haunt me as I review scenes from those days before I was old enough to understand that all Indian things would pass away.

I was born in a tepee on the Pine Ridge Reservation on June 11, 1870. The reservation had been established in the Dakota Territory a few years before I was born. My mother's name was "New Waw," meaning "White Swan." My father's name was "Wan-Ble-Sapa," which translated into "Black Eagle." I was called "To-Ka-Lu-Lu-Ta," or "Red Fox."

Our tepee was made from buffalo hides and I slept on a bearskin mat and a frame of willow boughs woven into a bed by my mother. The older children and their parents and grandparents slept on buffalo robes on the ground. The tepee was semicircular and varied from 22 to 33 feet wide. It was held up by poles that came to a peak at the top. In the winter it was banked around the bottom to keep out the cold, but was left open in the summer, giving us natural air-conditioning. We used buffalo chips for heating as well as for cooking when we could not find firewood.

We had four small tepees—one for cooking in bad weather; another for storing provisions; and the others to sleep in. Boys and girls never slept in the same tepees.

Small families were the rule among the Indians. They did not practice birth control, and abortions were unknown. The population was kept down by the naturalness of their environment; by the mothers nursing their babies longer than civilized women do; and by the absence of men while on the warpath, or on long hunting and trapping trips in quest of food. But more significant than anything else, sex was not a dominating compulsion with them. They did not drive nature in that, or in any other way, but let nature drive them.

At bedtime, if my father was away, my mother would tell me stories about her childhood and early life before the White man came. She did not know the exact year of her birth, but she thought it was about 1840. At that time, the country from the Mississippi River to the Western seaboard was populated mainly by Indian tribes. Their way of life had changed but little for centuries. They still hunted the buffalo on foot with bow and arrow. It was not until some years later that horses were used by the Indians in hunting, traveling, and warfare. Buffalo meat was their staple, always available food, but they supplemented it with fish, deer, partridge, quail, ducks, geese, berries, nuts, and fruits that grew in the wilderness. If they remained for months in one location, they planted squaw corn, beans, and squash. The food that was not eaten was dried in the sun and stored in buffalo skins for use while traveling, or in winter. The few White men who came among them were treated as friends. Years were to pass before they realized that they were threatened by an alien race, armed with superior weapons, intent upon seizing their land and ruthlessly destroying the wildlife upon which they depended for food, clothing, and shelter. Most of the buffalo that grazed on the plains when my mother was a girl had been shot by sportsmen, or killed by hunters for their hides and their tongues, which were pickled in salt and shipped to Eastern and Northern markets, where they were a delicacy when served in the White man's restaurant.

From my mother's bedtime stories I also learned much of the folklore that had come down from ancient times. She told me stories about birds and animals that lived on the plains and in the forests, why the Great Creator gave wings to the birds, the fawn its spots; the goat, elk, buffalo, and antelope their horns, the wolf the strong claws and teeth, and the rabbit his speed.

"Many years ago," she told me, "the Great Spirit roamed the earth. One night he was standing around a campfire telling about the many creatures he knew, and what he had done for them." My mother told of how the Great Creator had said, "I gave the birds feathers so they might fly away from enemies. I gave the mountain goat and buffalo their horns, the wolf his strong claws and teeth; the deer, elk, and antelope and rabbit their speed. . . ."

"Just then, a mother deer sped to his side closely followed by two fawn. 'O Spirit!' she said, 'you gave to me my speed, and to other creatures some means of protection, but how will my young fawn keep away from their enemies?'

"The Spirit replied, 'I will take care of the fawn. I shall change their color and give them spots so they will not be seen, and they will be safe while you and the other mothers are away. No animal shall ever find them because I will paint them like the leaves of the grass and shrubs. The spots will disappear as they grow and gain strength and speed.' "

She told me stories of how the Great Spirit had colored the birds, and gave each species a different call. She said, "The robin, oriole, and the cardinal get their color from the rising sun, the bluebird from the sky, parrots from the grass and leaves, the cockatoo's color from the moon and the snow, the peacock's from the rainbow.

"Before the White man came," she said, "and buffalo roamed over the land in great herds, we would follow them for the meat and hides that we needed. We camped along the streams, in valleys or in the forest for protection from enemies, and where there was wood for our fires."

She told me that when the tribes prepared to move, the women quickly took down the tepees, packed each one separately, and fastened it to a drag hitched to a pony. Other belongings and the small children were placed on this drag.

If the scouts found a good location where game and fish were plentiful, or wild berries were ready to be picked, the tribe would stay there for several months. In winter they built snow fences on the north side of their tepees, and gathered plenty of buffalo chips and firewood. When the women wanted to give their children a special treat, they served a tasty kind of cake called "wasna" which was made by mixing ground meats and berries.

The men spent their closed-in months making

bows and arrows, carving cooking utensils from the horns and bones of animals they had killed, or they fashioned elks' teeth and porcupine quills into the garments they wore at the Sun Dance and other ceremonies.

Among the Sioux, and most other tribes, the grandparents instructed the young in customs, laws, history, and government. They held council or study sessions for youth and passed on to them the information that had been transmitted to them by their grandparents. The sessions were like those held by Socrates, Plato, and Zeno on the porch and in the groves in ancient Greece. The students attended because they wanted to, not through compulsion, and no taxes had to be paid for tuition or teachers.

We were told that the Great Spirit looked after everything in nature; that he instructed the badger to burrow deeper ino the ground and the coyote to find shelter in the side of a hill when a cold winter was coming; and that he protected his animals by giving them heavier fur; and that he even looked after the ear of corn by giving it a thicker husk. We were never asked to bend our knees or to bow our heads in prayer, but we learned to look into the sky and reach out our hands for a blessing, or to ask forgiveness for some deviation from the paths of righteousness we were commanded to follow.

The Indians did not have a written language, so the older people had to be encyclopedias of knowledge that could be passed from one generation to another.

They knew the chants and rituals used in the dances and other ceremonies, and taught them to their pupils. One of the subjects they emphasized was the sign language, which was a universal medium of communication among the many tribes through which they could exchange commodities and hold councils with almost as much understanding as is achieved among the nations of the world today.

The average American boy of today would enjoy the privileges I had out there on the unspoiled prairie one hundred years ago. I was usually awake in time to see the sun rise. If the weather was warm, I went down to the river that flowed near our village and dipped water out of it with my hands for a drink, then plunged into it. The river came down out of the hills, ferrying leaves, blossoms, and driftwood. Fish could be seen in the pools formed near the rapids over which it rippled. Birds nested and flew among the banks, and occasionally I would see a coon or a fox in the brush. Hawks circled overhead, searching the ground for mice or other small animals for their breakfast, or to feed the young in their nests. There were never enough hours in a day to exhaust the pleasure of observing every living creature—from the orb spider spinning his magic and all but invisible web to the bald eagles on their bulky nests atop the tallest trees, teaching fledglings how to eject safely.

The halcyon days I like to remember were not by any means continuous. The Indians had not been completely subdued, and their lands were still wanted by the Whites. The Sioux were determined to keep the territory that was theirs by inheritance and treaty, and fierce battles were yet to be fought and lost while I still was a child. Our deep reverence for the invisible Creator of all things—the Great Spirit—was a sensitive influence in our struggle for survival; and we were to learn, as man has learned since the dawn of time, that religion is the most sensitive and intense thing that men fought over.

CHAPTER II

THE GREAT
SPIRIT

AMONG the American Indians there was a single concept of religion regardless of tribe or geographic location. They believed that the finite and infinite were expressions of one universal, absolute being that furnished guidelines for their morals and conduct, and motivated every living thing. They called this the Great Spirit.

Dr. John P. Harrington of the Smithsonian Institution, who conducted researches among many tribes and learned their languages, said that an Indian would not have been surprised had a tree opened its mouth and spoken to him, like the burning bush that spoke to Moses. The Indian viewed the sun as the greatest symbol of the Spirit he worshiped and always placed the opening of his tepee toward the east, where it first appeared in the morning. He did not worship the sun or set aside certain days specifically for devotion. His belief was integrated into his daily life, which it had to be, with his god always present and manifest in all things.

Gifted as the White man is with imagination and perception, and sometimes with compassion, he has never been able to understand why the Indians fought so fiercely to retain the Black Hills that rose in rugged outline above the grassy plains in the Dakota Territory. The Sioux believed that the Great Spirit had his abode in these hills even as the gods of ancient Greece lived on Mount Olympus. This belief had been etched in their consciousness through centuries. From where they lived in the land of the tall grass, they could see the Thunder Bird hovering above the high peaks, conjuring rain and snow and storms. They knew that spirits lived in the caves, and roamed among the forests of this paradise where they worshiped. These Black Hills were named by the Sioux Indians because the slopes were covered with thick pine forests which made them appear black when seen from the plains. The name would have been more accurate had they been called mountains, for their peaks reach up into the clouds and rugged cliffs jut out from their slopes. They have a primitive beauty that brings awe into the eyes of one beholding them for the first time. They have been compared to the famous Black Forest of Germany. Mount Harney, overlooking

Sylvan Lake, is 7,242 feet high, and there are a dozen other peaks that tower in sheer splendor above these ancient "hills."

Pictures painted on the walls of the caves up there were interpreted by the holy men as a guide on how to live. They were looked upon as the mystic language of the Great Spirit.

The springs that gushed from the cliffs and formed into pools were put there for man's use. They were the tears of the Great Spirit, and the healing waters were magic to the sick, the injured and crippled who went there for help; and where they often recovered miraculously. They filled their buffalo horns and rawhide bags with the healing water, and carried it back to their homes for the sick and those who were too old to journey to the waters.

Other tribes went to the wilderness health resort, and the Sioux did not molest them when they pitched their tepees, for they knew that no one would dare remain as permanent guests. The Great Spirit would punish them, or the Thunder Bird would wash them away in a flood. They hunted the deer and the elk and the bear which had been placed there in abundance by the Creator to provide meat and fur for his children.

The chiefs of the Sioux and other tribes held councils in the caves, and the medicine men went there often to commune, and to refresh and replenish their belief and reverence.

My mother and father and my grandparents went there often, taking me with them; and I can remember the feeling of reverence which I experienced as I bathed in the Tears of the Great Spirit.

Many moons before the White man came, the Indians knew of the gold that underlay the hills and mountains. They felt that this too was sacred, and should be used only in religious ceremonies, and never sold or used in trade.

It was not for the gold or for their hunting grounds that the Indians fought the miners, squatters, speculators, and blue-coated soldiers who invaded their territory like a swarm of locusts; but they fought in defense of this shrine that had been sacred to them from time immemorial. And that was the reason the Indians refused to sell the Black Hills, even when the government offered them $16,000,000. They might have sold their hunting grounds, but they could not sell the campsite and domicile of their ancient god and protector.

The Indian was going about his own private business in the part of the world the Creator had given him when an ambitious sailor from Madrid picked the time lock on his paradise. He had identified his god in the weeds and mountains and sky. He did not think he was any closer to this creative and protective force than the animals and birds, or the wind that blew around his tepee.

To present this god as Nature is like trying to immobilize a wave by driving a nail into it. The Indian was aware of the statutes written in the Book of Nature, meaning that gave him reverence and serenity; but the Great Spirit was something he could not see. It existed only in symbology and in the invisible outposts of his consciousness. His concept of divinity was inconceivable to the strict religionists who came to his landed paradise in 1492. This native American was condemned as a pagan and a savage, and unless he walked out on the Great Spirit and bowed to the God of the White man, he was no more important than an animal.

The most interesting discussion I have had on this subject was back in the 1920s when I was interviewed by a newspaperwoman in Philadelphia. She wanted to know if I still worshiped the Great Spirit. This was after a long and pleasant discussion. I did not answer her directly, but opened my briefcase and took out a copy of the speech that Chief Red Jacket of the Iroquois made at a conference after a missionary addressed his tribe at a meeting in Buffalo, New York, in 1805. I always carried reference material with me, including this speech. I handed it to the woman and asked her to read the following paragraphs from it as an answer to her question:

"Friend and brother, it was the will of the Great Spirit that we should meet together this day. He

[14]

orders all things, and he has given us a fine day for our council. He has taken his garment from before the sun, and caused it to shine with brightness upon us; our eyes are opened, and we see clearly; our ears are unstopped, and we have been able to hear distinctly the words that you have spoken; for all these favors we thank the Great Spirit and Him only. . . .

"Brother, listen to what we say. There was a time when our forefathers owned this great land. Their seats extended from the rising to the setting sun. The Great Spirit had made it for use by the Indians. He had created the buffalo, the deer, and other animals for food. He made the bear and the beaver, and the skins served for clothing. He had scattered them over the country, and taught us how to take them. He had caused the earth to produce corn for bread.

"All this he had done for his Red children because he loved them. If we had any disputes about hunting grounds they were generally settled without the shedding of blood.

"But an evil day came upon us; your forefathers crossed the great waters, and landed on this island. Their numbers were small; they found friends, not enemies; they told us they had fled from their own country for fear of wicked men, and came here to enjoy their religion. They asked for a small seat; we took pity upon them, granted their request, and they sat down among us. We gave them corn and meat; they gave us poison in return.

"The White people had now found our country, tidings were carried back, and more came among us; yet we did not fear them. We took them to be friends; they called us brothers, we believed them, and gave them a larger seat. At length their numbers had greatly increased, and they wanted more land, they wanted our country. Our eyes were opened and our minds became uneasy. Wars took place; Indians were hired to fight against Indians; and many of our people were destroyed. They also brought strong liquor among us.

"Brother, our seats were once large, and yours were very small. You now have become a great people, and we scarcely have a place left to spread our blankets. You have our country, but you are not satisfied, you want to force your religion upon us.

"Brother, continue to listen. You say that you are sent to instruct us how to worship the Great Spirit agreeably to His mind, and if we do not take hold of the religion which you White people teach, we shall be unhappy hereafter; you say you are right and we are lost. How do you know this to be true? We understand that your religion is written in a book. If it was intended for us as well as for you, why has not the Great Spirit given it to us, and not only to us, but why did He not give us, and our forefathers, the knowledge of that book, with the means of understanding it rightly? We know only what you tell us. How shall we know to believe, being so often deceived by the White people?

"Brother, you say there is but one way to worship and serve the Great Spirit. If there be but one religion, why do you White people differ so much about it? Why not all agree as you can read the book? . . .

"Brother, the Great Spirit has made all of us, but he has made a great difference between his White and Red children. He has given us a different complexion and different customs. To you he has given the arts; to these he has not opened our eyes. We know these things to be true. Since He has made so great a difference between us in other things, why may we not conclude that He has given us a different religion according to our understanding? The Great Spirit does right. He knows what is best for His children. We are satisfied.

"Brother, you now have heard our answer to your talk. As we are going to part, we will take you by the hand, and hope the Great Spirit will protect you on your journey, and return you safe to your friends."

The chiefs and other Indians drew near the minister, but he arose hastily from his seat and told them there was no fellowship between the religion of God and the works of the Devil, and that he could not shake their hands.

After reading this, the reporter said she wanted to copy the paragraphs she had read, and I waited patiently until she had finished. Then she looked into my face and said, "Your religion is not much different from what many Christians believe. The Great Spirit and God must be brothers—if they are not the same."

She asked me about the dances of the Indians, and whether or not they were ceremonials. I told her they were just as when David danced "with all his might" and his musicians played a concert before the Lord.

I do not know if this interview ever appeared in print, but I believe that I was able to open the mind of one person to the perception that truth is sometimes buried under falsehood, and that religion ultimately settles down to a contact and conflict between man and his Maker.

Nonsectarian, impartial historians have been tolerant in telling about the primitive Americans and their conquerors. Many of the early missionaries were eloquent in their praise. The Reverend Mr. C. Van Dusen, who spent time with the Ojibway people, says:

"The Indian character, in its unadulterated grandeur, is most admirable and attractive. Before it is polluted by the pernicious example of others—the demoralizing and debasing influence of wicked White men—the genuine North American pagan presents to the world the most noble specimen of the natural man that can be found on the face of the earth."

Bishop Henry Benjamin Whipple, of Minnesota, described the Indian, after a lifetime of association, in these words:

"The North American Indian is the noblest type of a heathen man on the earth. He recognizes a Great Spirit; he believes in immortality; he has a quick intellect; he is a clear thinker; he is brave and fearless; and until betrayed, he is true to his plighted faith. He has a passionate love for his children, and counts it a joy to die for his people. Our most terrible wars have been with the noblest types of the Indians and with men who had been the White man's friends. Nicolet said the Sioux were the finest type of wild men he had ever seen."

The Jesuit Father J. F. Lafitau, widely recognized for his missionary work among primitive Americans, described the Medicine Lodge of the Sioux as a " 'true Church of God,' and we have no right to stamp it out."

One of America's leading military men, General Nelson A. Miles, who directed wars against the Indians for fifteen years, appraised them as follows in his memoirs:

"History can show no parallel to the heroism and fortitude of the American Indians in the 200 years fight during which they contested inch by inch the possession of their country against a foe infinitely better equipped, with inexhaustible resources and in overwhelming numbers. Had they been equal in numbers, history would have had a very different story to tell."

Strange indeed it is that the army officers did not sense this when they were detailed to the Indian country to try to civilize them. Stranger, still, is that the government did not send schoolteachers rather than powder and bullets. The missionaries who preceded the soldiers realized that the Indians had many excellent qualities and high ideals. If the army officers could have realized that fact, history would have a different story to record, and the government would have been saved the chagrin it must bear for the unfair treatment it accorded its native Americans. Be it said to the credit of some officers that they came to understand the culture and customs of the Indian people, and often befriended them.

After his retirement, General Miles became their champion and struggled valiantly to safeguard their rights, and to protect them from wars and persecution. I became well acquainted with him and often conferred with him on policies and legislation affecting the Indians.

It is said that first impressions are lasting, and this proved true with the Indians who gained their first knowledge of the White people through association with the soldiers. While the officers of that day were educated and disciplined, the average enlisted man was addicted to drinking, gambling, and lewdness. They were far removed from the sobering influences of church, home, and women. The Sioux were shocked to hear these palefaces flippantly use the name of the Great Spirit in jest, or carry on licentious conversations. No tribe of Indians has a word with which to take the name of the Great Spirit in vain, nor do they have curse words such as the White man has.

No other race of people has a deeper love of family and home than the Sioux. They never punished their children by whipping or beating them. Many White people slap their children, snatch them by their ears, and drag them by the arms, or beat them with straps and sticks. I once heard an old Indian remark after seeing a White man beat a little boy, "We love our children and beat our horses; the White man loves his horses and beats his children." Only recently American educators have recognized the harmful effects that come from manhandling children.

Indian children were taught that respect and obedience were due their parents because of the sacrifices they made. The child was taught that when he was weak and could not care for himself, the parents were strong, but as they grew weak the child grew strong and must care for them. When boys needed discipline they were denied the right to play war games, practice with bow and arrow, or track an animal to its den. Girls were denied privileges of playing with their dolls, helping their mothers prepare a meal around a campfire, or stitching hardened berries or shells on garments. The punishments were always negative. They were denied something they loved which they could comprehend mentally; but not abused physically, something that had no association with their offense.

Family ties have always been so strong among the Sioux that they are slow to see wrong in the conduct of a close relative, and no sacrifice is too great to make for a child. Indian mothers have been known to sell their best bed, or even the cookstove, in order to raise money to send a child to school away from home.

Only recently has the White race learned that women are intelligent enough to be trusted with the ballot. This the Indians recognized in primitive times. Among many tribes the Indian women selected the men who served on their councils. If one of these officials misbehaved, the women could recall him. They also had complete authority in the upbringing of children until they were seven years old; and they sometimes served on the warpath, stampeding the enemy's horses and decoying soldiers from the main line of battle.

An Indian once said, "We long ago learned that some women are wiser than some men. If the woman produced the chief, she must be about as wise as the chief."

Indians do not have to be reminded to feed the hungry, clothe the poor, or to give shelter to those in need. They do it instinctively and sincerely, and with pleasure. They visit the sick and afflicted, and are sympathetic to those who suffer misfortune or disaster.

The White people of America failed to realize until it was almost too late that it was necessary to conserve wildlife, but as far back as history can trace the Indians have been aware of that need. They killed only what they needed for food. Many a White hunter killed for the sordid pleasure derived from destroying life; and even today it is only by drastic laws that the annihilation of endangered species is prevented.

The worth and character of a race may be judged by the actions of its soldiers in line of battle, and here the Sioux had no superiors, and few equals. In his own lost cause, he faced death courageously; and in the World Wars I and II, he stood by the side of his White brother unflinching and calm and fought for the same rights that his forefathers fought for—the land he loved, the freedom he shared and was ready to die for. I can report this in all modesty for in 1917 I went to Washington to call upon Secretary of War Newton D. Baker to offer the services of the Indians. These are the words I spoke: "From all over the West we now stand ready—50,000 Indians between the ages of seventeen and fifty-five. We beg of you to give us the right to fight. We guarantee to you, sir, our hearts could be for no better cause than to fight for the land we love, and for the freedom we share. Let us fight as one division. If we are not qualified to go to France then let us guard 1,400 miles along the borders of the Rio Grande. We guarantee you, sir, no enemy will trespass, pillage, or destroy a sprig of grass on the eastern side of the Rio Grande."

Secretary Baker's reply was: "I cannot accept your offer to fight as one division, nor can I accept the age of seventeen to fifty-five, but I will accept your offer to serve in any branch of the armed services where we see fit, but from the ages of twenty-one to forty-five."

The war records show that 17,330 Indians were in World War I; 8,047 Indians went to France; 1,032 were killed or died from influenza.

In World War II, 39,000 Indian boys and girls responded to the call of arms. They served in all branches of the armed forces.

Major General Clarence Tinker, a full-blood

Osage, was killed in 1942 in the Midway Island battle. His son, a major, was killed at Casablanca in North Africa.

Inaan Hayse, a Pima Indian, helped raise the flag on Iwo Jima, and many more Indians stood hand in hand and fought in air, on land and sea. Again, they fought in Korea for the freedom of our country, and for their fellow man. They were united under the flag of the United States of America, and my prayer is: "Long may it wave over all men as brothers."

CHAPTER III

"AS LONG AS THE SUN SHINES"

I NOW have to turn back to trails that were made and events that occurred before I was born when the Sioux still hunted and fished unmolested in their ancient homeland on the Western plains and mountains. From my grandparents I learned the folklore, rituals, and customs of my ancestors, but here I am concerned with the sinister shadow that spread over the land in 1865 when the government decided to build a road from Fort Laramie deep into the Indian Territory.

When news of this reached Red Cloud, chief of the Oglalas, the largest tribe of the Sioux Nation, he protested to Washington that building the road would scatter the buffalo upon which the Indian depended for food and clothing. He reminded the officials that the land belonged to the Indians, but neither his pleas nor his protests could move ambitious men who were demanding that the territory be opened for exploitation.

Red Cloud had always been a peaceful man willing to reason together with his White brothers, counseling negotiations in times of trouble. He was not in the hereditary line that would have made him a chief, but he rose to power through the strength of his personality and his service to the tribe. His attitude began to harden when his father died from vile liquor obtained from the Whites a few years before; and now the action of the government transformed him into a bitter, warlike figure. Almost overnight he became the most influential leader of the tribes and subtribes that comprised the Sioux Nation. The mass of Indians numbering around 35,000 looked upon him as a commander who could lead them in war, and prevent the White man from invading their sacred lands.

When, as the Indians had expected, a detachment of troops and road-builders moved into the wilderness and established a camp, Red Cloud's spies were watching, and a company of warriors were waiting to attack. Red Cloud held them in check until a detail of workmen carrying axes and saws left the camp. When they started cutting the timber, the Indians surrounded them, and they surrendered without resistance. They were held prisoners for two weeks until Red Cloud was informed that a commission was on the way from Washington to see him. He released the prisoners, but refused to meet with the commissioners, for he felt that they did not have the authority of a council. The commission returned to Washington and reported that the Indians were in a warlike mood.

The government acted quickly and called a council at Fort Laramie. Red Cloud and other chiefs of the Sioux attended. While in session, Colonel Harry Carrington rode in with a detachment of soldiers and announced that he had orders from the government to build a string of forts all the way to the Black Hills. When the announcement was made, Red Cloud was addressing the council. He was stunned into momentary silence, then he turned to Carrington in anger. His words are not recorded, but the colonel assured him that the forts would be built—by force if necessary.

Red Cloud picked up his rifle and stalked from the room followed by the other chiefs. This was the signal for war. Red Cloud sent a call to all the Sioux tribes and appealed for help from Cheyennes who occupied the adjoining lands, and soon he had an army of 4,000 warriors assembled.

In the meantime Carrington had settled down in a camp on Piney Creek and started to build the first fort. Red Cloud's troops were deployed in the nearby hills waiting for the signal to attack. The chief waited until the timbermen, protected by troops, began cutting trees a few miles from their camp. Then he gave the signal and a band of his warriors attacked and killed the entire detachment of 81 men.

Other assaults were made against men and troops who strayed away from the protection of their camp, and Carrington was restrained from building a single fort. He informed his superiors that the task was proving to be impossible because of the opposition of the Indians.

During the months this conflict was going on not a single wagon train was permitted to enter the Sioux Territory. The warriors remained at their posts expecting the arrival of government troops in force, but they did not come. Instead, the government sent a commission to come to terms with Red Cloud. He and other chiefs of the Sioux and Cheyennes met them at Fort Laramie early in January, 1868.

At that meeting, discussions included a proposal to buy the land of the Sioux, but Red Cloud refused arbitrarily, and told the commissioners that the Indians would fight for their ancient hunting grounds and sacred lands until the last one was killed if necessary. Convinced that the Indians would follow Red Cloud into a major war, and that no persuasion or offer of money could change his decision, they agreed to redefine the Sioux Territory and give them a treaty that would assure it to them "as long as the sun shines and the grass grows."

The treaty further stipulated that the country of the North Platte, through the Black Hills to the summits of the Big Horn Mountains, be considered to be unceded Indian Territory and that no White person would be permitted to settle upon or occupy any portion of it without the consent of the Indians. The government also agreed to abandon its construction projects and withdraw all troops in the area.

The treaty was satisfactory to Red Cloud, but he refused to sign it until the garrison at Piney Creek left. He was waiting there with his warriors when the last of the troops departed, then set fire to the buildings that had been erected there. Before they passed from view beyond the hills, the smoke was spiraling toward the sky.

Red Cloud had promised to disband his warriors as soon as the government withdrew its troops and completely discarded the road and forts projects in the territory. He kept his word and never again engaged in war, but came to realize that the Indians were doomed as a people. They could not fight a successful war against the combined forces of the government and the hordes of White settlers determined to possess the land.

The treaty had been signed at Fort Laramie on November 6, 1868, and after sending his warriors back to their families and homes Red Cloud stepped down from leadership, and his name does not appear in the chronicles of conflict that followed, even in the war of 1876 or the Messiah Outbreak in 1890. He spent his last years in a house given to him by the government, on the Pine Ridge Reservation, and there he died in 1909 in his eighty-seventh year.

For a few years after the treaty was signed, the government established an agency in the Sioux

Territory and peace reigned, but it was an armed peace with frequent killings as White traders, adventurers, and speculators went there hoping to gain wealth through their dealings with the Indians. The government sent small detachments of troops to the territory in order to expel the invaders and honor its treaty obligations; but the troops were too few, and the adventurers too many. It was like trying to put out a prairie fire with sprinkling cans.

Soon thereafter General George A. Custer and the Seventh Cavalry arrived in the Black Hills, reportedly to make a military survey, but in reality to investigate conditions between the Whites and the Indians. One day he discovered flecks of gold on the shoes of his horse, which confirmed persisting reports and rumors that rich deposits of this metal underlay the Black Hills.

General Custer reported his findings to Washington and geological and mining experts were sent there to make a survey. When they came out of the hills the fate of the Sioux was assured. The surveyors had indisputable evidence that gold existed in abundance there.

The news, which was flashed over the "talking wires" and printed in newspaper headlines, was discussed in financial circles, and in saloons and dance halls where miners, adventurers, and land-grabbers gathered. Within days a horde of fortune hunters was heading toward the glistening frontier in the Black Hills. They arrived in the Sioux country on horseback, in wagon trains, and on foot—some carrying only pack sacks and shovels. They prospected in the hills, along the streams, and in the mountains where the Indians hunted elk, bear, and deer. They cut down timber for campfires, staked out claims, shot the wild game for sport and food, and began building homes and starting settlements.

At first the Indians were bewildered, but they soon realized that not only were their hunting grounds being overrun but the sacred temples in the high hills where they worshiped and found health were being despoiled, and the Great Spirit was calling out for their help.

CHAPTER IV

THE SUN
GOES DOWN

STORED among the unforgettable memories of my childhood is a moment of time that has become a part of history. It was on an early morning in 1876. The sun was lighting the Big Horn Mountains with the colors of dawn. My mother was moving about in our tepee, and I was standing outside facing the west. I knew that fighting was going on up there among the crags and cliffs, for I had heard the firing of guns the day before, and there had been warlike activities in the village where we lived. More than 6,000 women, children, and old men were there. All of the able-bodied men and boys over fourteen years old had gone up into the mountains, some riding their ponies, others on foot. They were armed with rifles, pistols, and hunting knives. I had no comprehension of the scope of the battle that was going on, but I wished that I could be with the warriors. I was later to learn that they were engaged in the greatest battle ever fought between the White man and the Indians.

The memory of that morning when I stood at the break of dawn and the unfolding of history tempered my life and tested my spirit as I witnessed the downfall of the Sioux Nation and the decay of the ideals, customs, and religion which held it together. During that day the village was subdued. The women and old men gathered in groups and gazed toward the mountains where the smoke of battle could be seen floating above the hills and peaks, and the exploding of the big guns mounted on wagons could be heard. Prayers to the Great Spirit were on the lips of wives whose husbands were up there, and girls whose lovers might never return. The children, caught in the shadow of the tragedy, were repressed, and even the dogs slunk about as if reflecting the worries and behavior of the people.

Once that day I saw the great medicine man Sitting Bull mounting a horse in front of a tepee. For a few moments he sat there looking toward the mountains, holding out his hands as if appealing to the Great Spirit. He wore buckskin moccasins, trousers, and shirt. The sides of the trousers were fringed and the shirt was decorated with porcupine quills. I especially remember his face, for it was unpainted. I had seen him before, but never like that. His features were stern and he seemed unaware of those around him. His broad shoulders slumped slightly, but I was impressed with a man of great strength and superhuman power. I watched as he slowly rode away into the foothills. There are writers who have said he took part in the battle that day, but my mother told me that he had a secret place in the mountains where he communed alone with the Great Spirit.

The story of what happened that day has been told and retold, in many ways, by historians and fiction writers. It is a twisted, tangled web of facts, errors, suppositions, and poetic license, enshrining General George Armstrong Custer in the notebooks of time, and in the Hall of Fame with other American heroes and martyrs. It was the day in which this storied general, known among the Indians as "Yellow Hair," fought and was killed for what he considered the honor of his country. The battle is called "Custer's Last Stand." It was described as the "Indian Massacre" in newspaper articles of that time, and later in magazines and books by writers who continued to regard the Red man as a barbarian and a savage.

What I report here is distilled from my own memories, which are vivid, and from what my father and my uncle, Crazy Horse, later told me about the fighting which took place among the cliffs and on the banks of the Little Big Horn River. The battle could more accurately be designated as "The Last Stand of the Sioux Indians," for they were nearing the end of their existence as an independent, reverent, and powerful race. Their ancient hunting grounds had been invaded by White men armed with guns, and already only a scattering of buffalo remained on the plains and in the Black Hills. The treaty which Red Cloud negotiated was nothing more than a scrap of paper in the files of the Indian Bureau. The sacred mountains where they went to commune with the Great Spirit and to seek his physical and spiritual medicine were being mutilated by the pickaxes and the blasting powder of miners. Overnight, towns were springing up with noisy saloons and dancehalls where painted women, traders, land-grabbers, and gamblers congregated to peddle their wares.

The man the government was depending upon, more than anyone else, to bring a semblance of order to this fantastic gold frontier was General Custer. He had led many skirmishes against the Indians. A few years before he had attacked a peaceful Cheyenne village at daybreak and killed a number of unarmed women and children. This exploit is recorded in Indian Bureau files in Custer's words as "The Battle of the Washita," even though the Indians did not fire a single shot. The word "Washita" was widely used by the Plains Indians to denote the White man.

The immediate events that preceded the death of Custer began when a delegation of Indians on the Standing Rock Reservation went to see Major James McLaughlin and reported that traders were robbing them of their furs and hides. Major McLaughlin was one of the few White men on the frontier at that time who understood the character of the Sioux and sympathized with them. He had written a book entitled *My Friend the Indian*. He did not doubt the truth of what the delegates told him, for his suspicions had been aroused by reports from other sources. He immediately sent word to all the posts that everyone must have a permit, bearing his signature, before they could trade on the reservation. An unscrupulous veterinarian stole one of the permit forms and forged the major's signature on it. Then he and three other men, named Brown, Bayon, and Ball, started trading with the Indians.

One day an Indian named Eagle Shield was trying to make them pay for some furs they had bought from him, and they paid with a bullet which killed Eagle Shield. A small Indian girl saw the shooting and told her uncle Rain-in-the-Face, who was chief of the Buffalo Clan to which I belong.

Rain-in-the-Face mounted his pony and rode out of the village, following the trail of the men who had killed Eagle Shield. He found them making camp for the night. He shot and killed Bayon, the veterinarian, and Ball, but Brown got away.

A few days later, while traveling through the area on his way to Fort Sturgis, Colonel Sterling found the bodies of the three men and the moccasin tracks of the man who had killed them. He informed the War Department and orders were dispatched to Fort Lincoln, which was located where Bismarck, North Dakota, is today, to apprehend the slayer. General Custer was the commanding officer there, and he sent his brother Captain Tom Custer and Lieutenant Calahan to the Standing Rock Reservation to investigate, but they could not learn anything from the Indians. For eighteen months the killing remained a mystery to the military officers as well as to the Indians.

The first inkling of who avenged the murder of Eagle Shield came one morning at the reservation agency when Indians were drawing their monthly supplies. Rain-in-the-Face was seen telling a friend, in the sign language, that he had killed the traders and was the man being hunted by the soldiers.

The man who heard him tell of the killing was Charlie Reynolds, a half-blood Indian whose father was an officer in the Seventh Cavalry, and he immediately sent word to him. A few days later Captain Custer arrived at the reservation, placed Rain-in-the-Face under arrest, and took him to Fort Lincoln. On the way, the chief was beaten and spurred by Custer and the troopers who accompanied him. As they arrived at the stockade, Rain-in-the-Face told Custer that if he ever got the chance he would cut his heart out because of the treatment he had received. He was placed in jail with five other prisoners, but within a week they were freed by deserters from the Seventh Cavalry.

While being held at the fort, Chief Rain-in-the-Face heard that President Grant had ordered the army to stop all the Indians from hunting buffalo. This inflamed the waning spirits of the Sioux. Even though they were receiving rations from the government, they still depended upon the buffalo for the fur and hides they needed for clothing, moccasins, robes, and tepees.

On June 8, 1876, the great medicine man and prophet Sitting Bull called a council of the Sioux and Cheyenne chiefs. Among those who attended were Crazy Horse and my father Black Eagle of the Sioux, and Two Moons of the Cheyennes. Sitting Bull asked, "Shall we die of hunger and our children want for clothing from the hides of the buffalo?" They made plans to go to the Big Horn Basin where buffalo, elk, deer, and bear could still be found.

At that time I was six years old, but even today after 500 moons have passed, I can remember the long, hot, dusty journey with scores of ponies struggling over the parched land dragging our tepees and other supplies. I remember the nights of camping along streams where we refreshed ourselves, and the campfires when we roasted jerky, or ate fresh meat that our warriors brought into camp. I remember too the vast mystery that filled my child's mind as a new enchanting world opened to me where the wind and the stars were companions of eternity, and the primitive beauty of nature was still reflected in the clear running waters and on the lofty peaks of the mountains. Had I known that the sun was going down for the Sioux, and that this would be the last hopeful pilgrimage they would ever make, I would have wept as even today I sometimes weep in memory's secret chamber.

Our journey finally ended in the foothills of the Big Horn Mountains, where we set up our village in a kind of amphitheater. The followers of Sitting Bull and Crazy Horse, who had refused to give up their freedom and live on the reservation, were already encamped there. The Cheyennes had gathered in another protected site about three miles from us. The Indians were expecting trouble, and were prepared for it. Their scouts had reported that Custer had left Fort Lincoln and was on the way to the Big Horn with his Seventh Cavalry.

The first trouble started when a band of Cheyenne warriors, coming from the reservation at Red Lodge on the Tongue River in Montana, met and defeated a troop of soldiers commanded by General George Crook. When Custer heard of this, he was quoted as saying, "They won't force me to retreat. I will show the boys and the President who can whip the Indians." He may have been thinking of the time he had killed 52 Cheyenne women and children on the Washita River when not one able-bodied man was in the village.

Custer was at odds with President Grant because of trouble he had several months earlier after testifying against Secretary of War William W. Belknap during a hearing that implicated the President's brother Orval in scandals of the Indian Bureau, although he added nothing to what the brother had already confessed to under oath. He had been removed from command, but was restored to duty through the intervention of Brigadier General Alfred H. Terry.

On June 22 our scouts reported that his troops had set up camp about twenty miles from our village, just eight miles from where destiny was waiting in ambush for him. The fight that followed, as I have been able to construct it from memory, from what my father and others told me, and from the official records, comes into focus as follows:

My uncle, Chief Crazy Horse, who scorned life on the reservation, had won a place of leadership among all the Sioux. Many of the Indians lived with him on lands that had not yet come under complete government control. During the previous winter, his band of warriors had been surprised in a dawn attack by forces under Generals Crook and Reynolds, and lost their horses. In a blinding snowstorm that followed, the Indians managed to stampede the herd and recovered their mounts.

Crazy Horse was in charge of at least 3,000 well-armed and seasoned Sioux and Cheyenne warriors. Massed against him were the combined troops of Custer, Crook, and Reynolds. These were deployed in various strategic locations in the hills, valleys, and mountains. Custer, who was directing the strategy, had given orders for an attack at four o'clock. However, the first contact occurred two hours before when a band of the Sioux, directed by Black Hawk and my father, Black Eagle, blocked an advance by Reynolds. About that time, other warriors halted a company of bluecoats at the Rose Bud River and drove them across the river. A pack train carrying supplies to Custer's men was attacked and scattered.

It is reported that Custer's main strategy was to attack our defenseless village and demoralize the warriors. The records of his previous actions lend support to this belief, as did statements by my father and Crazy Horse in the days following the battle. My father told me that the Indians were prepared for this, and when Custer ordered his men to march toward the river, which lay between them and the village, Crazy Horse had the area surrounded, and Indians stalked unseen behind Custer's men to stop them from retreating. When he neared the river, Custer ordered his troops to dismount and advance on foot, leaving their horses with sentries. He had gone only a few hundred yards when he saw that the Indians were closing in, and he ordered his bugler to sound a call for the sentries to bring up the horses. But it was too late! A group of Indian women who had accompanied their men into battle, as they often did, had stampeded the animals. Dismayed and apparently sensing an ambush, he hastened to command the bugler to signal for a retreat. But again he was too late, for the warriors had caught him and his men in a trap and a rain of bullets hit them from every side, as Crazy Horse and his men closed the ring around them. Some tried to swim the river or escape into the hills, but there was no avenue for either retreat or escape. Only one man, Curley the Crow, survived that battle. He was the last man to see Custer alive. Years later, he told me that Custer went down in a hail of bullets with his staff grouped around him. I asked how he managed to escape, and he said he took off his soldier's coat when the fighting started and lay down and played dead. After dark, he made his way to General Reynolds' camp and told him that Custer and all his men had been killed. Curley the Crow died in 1918 at Hardin, Montana.

The Indians reported that 35 of their warriors were killed. Custer had 261 men with him, but the forces of Crook and Reynolds also were under his command.

What actually happened after that Battle of the Little Big Horn is not clearly defined in the pages, or on the monuments of history. Some of it is depicted on tombstones, but most of what happened in those postmortem days is viewed with uninterest by writers. The battle did not end when Custer and his troops were destroyed, for the Indians attacked General Crook's company and defeated it decisively.

However, by that time they had depleted their ammunition and what they had taken from Custer's men. The forces of Generals Crook and Reynolds were still intact, and Crazy Horse realized that more government troops, including those under the command of General Miles, would be rushed to the area as soon as word of Custer's death reached Washington. He called the chiefs into council and they decided to disband and withdraw from the mountain battlefield.

I can remember when the Sioux warriors returned to our village. Only a few were missing or wounded. Some of the Indians sought to escape into Canada, but the majority decided to return to the reservation. Crazy Horse took his band to a remote part of the territory where enough buffalo remained then to provide them with food and clothing; and Sitting Bull fled to another region accompanied by about 400 men, women, and children. Within two or three hours the tepees in our village were taken down, packed on drags, and we were moving out of the Big Horn Basin toward the Black Hills and the plains. Fearing pursuit, we traveled for a night and day as fast as the ponies could go, pausing only for water.

There was no joy for anyone in this pilgrimage, for the people were made silent with sadness. Their warriors had killed "Yellow Hair," a hated enemy, but that was a small morsel to rejoice over when they thought of the dreary future that awaited them on the reservation, where scarcely a buffalo remained and the Washita were plundering their land, desecrating the forested temples and the "tears of the Great Spirit" in their sacred hills.

We arrived back at the reservation without mishap, and had just settled into our old routine when we learned that General Miles had been sent to the territory to prevent further uprisings. He did not go to the reservation, but his troops harassed the villages of Sitting Bull and Crazy Horse, and kept their men from hunting. Hungry and ragged, the Indians fled from the troops. There was no place where they could find security and peace. General Miles counseled Sitting Bull to take his people to the reservation, where they would be provided with food and clothing by the government. This only aroused the anger of the indomitable medicine man, who was one of the greatest characters the White man ever encountered in his conflicts and associations with the Indians. He told General Miles that the Indians had never fought an aggressive war against the White man, and that they would lay down their arms and stop fighting if the troops were withdrawn from their country and their posts abandoned.

General Miles responded to the demands by asserting that nothing less than an unconditional surrender by the Indians would be accepted. This inflamed Sitting Bull still more, and he exclaimed, "Almighty God made me an Indian, but not an agency Indian."

That terminated the conference and Sitting Bull returned to his village; but he expected an attack, and was preparing to leave when General Miles' horsemen were seen galloping toward the village. The Indians fled, leaving their tepees and all their supplies. Facing inconceivable suffering and hardship, Sitting Bull decided to take his harassed band to Canada. All the way he was pursued, but he kept out of firing range and finally crossed the border. There, in the black pine forests, they found refuge. But there was no happiness for Sitting Bull and no peace in his spirit. The memory of the wrongs that had been inflicted upon his people and to the Great Spirit of his ancestors tormented him, and from those thoughts there was no escape.

General Miles was especially eager to round up Crazy Horse and his followers. The chief had about 2,000 people with two or three hundred trained warriors in his band. The two forces met in several encounters, but the Indians, weakened and dispirited, had to keep moving to escape the persistent, well-fed and well-clothed cavalrymen. At last Crazy Horse accepted the reality that nothing could be done to restore the past, and he agreed to a conference with the general. Bitterness crept into his words as he recounted the crimes the White man and his soldiers had committed against the Indians. General Miles listened patiently and thanked Crazy Horse when he said his people would go to the reservation.

The troops escorted the dejected men, women, and children to the agency on the Pine Ridge Reservation and into the custody of the nation that had stolen their land and brought them to their knees in abject and humiliating submission.

In previous years I had seldom seen my great uncle, but after he went to the reservation he occasionally visited our tepee, and I remember listening to talks between him and my father. He was always kind, but the tragedy that had overpowered the people he loved and fought so valiantly to save had dimmed the light that once flamed in his courageous spirit, and the imprint was written on his face.

Death came to Crazy Horse when he was less than forty years old. He had left the reservation and was on his way to an army post seeking help for his wife, who was suffering from tuberculosis, when a troop of soldiers intercepted him. He had left the reservation without permission, and so great was his reputation that the word spread that he had escaped and was planning to organize another assault. When he told the soldiers his mission, they allowed him to proceed, but went with him. Once they reached the post and escorted him into a building, he knew it was a jailhouse. Enraged by the treachery, he drew a knife from his jacket and furiously attacked the soldiers who surrounded him. He was overpowered and beaten to the floor where he lay struggling when a soldier plunged a bayonet into his back, bringing almost instant death.

His body was claimed by his parents and taken away in a *travois*, drawn by a pony. No one except his family ever knew where he was laid to rest.

My mother told me the story of how Crazy Horse was killed. Others have reported the details in different ways, but this I am certain is substantially true. His death was a final, fatal blow against the Sioux and, like the assassination a few years later of Sitting Bull, has been written in the blood used to record the great tragedies of history.

CHAPTER V

THE GHOST DANCE

BY the year 1888 the Indian was a forlorn pilgrim on earth. His culture and spiritual heritage were in ruins. He was shrinking like the animals of an endangered species in the captivity of a zoo. His zoo was a reservation, but there was neither cowardice nor fear in his attitude, only regrets trapped in the pathways of memory. He was bewildered by the mysticism of the White man's religion and the Messiah who had come to the earth nearly 2,000 years before to show mankind the trail that led to heaven. His belief in the ancestral god of his people was faltering, and only a miracle, like the one enacted along the Sea of Galilee, could restore his faith.

Thus, in 1888, when it was reported that a Paiute Indian had been transported to heaven in a vision, and that the Great Spirit was coming back to the world to drive the White man out of America and restore the wilderness, the Indians were emotionally and physically prepared to believe him. In their secret prayers, they had been appealing for the Messiah.

The man who proclaimed these revelations was named Wovoka. The vision had come to him when the sun was darkened by an eclipse. He said that the Great Spirit had told him that vast herds of buffalo would be created and turned loose on the plains; that the deer, elk, and antelope would return, the sanctuary in the Black Hills be restored, and the White man flee back to the land from where he came.

Wovoka was born near Walker's Lake, Nevada, and lived there for several years with a White family. He was scarcely known until the vision came to him. He informed his friends among the Paiutes about his experience, and they were impressed by his sincerity and inspirational fervor. He told them of awakening in heaven and seeing many of those who had died, living together in joy and happiness. He quoted the Great Spirit as telling him to return to his people and counsel them to "be good and love one another, have no quarreling, and live in peace with the Whites, and put away all practices that savored of war; and if they obeyed him, they would be reunited with their friends and relatives in the other world."

Wovoka told them too that the Great Spirit wanted them to dance again with the enthusiasm they had in the old days, only this would be a spiritual outpouring of their adoration for the one who was returning to relieve them of their troubles and suffering. Wovoka instructed them in rites that were to accompany this new dance.

The depressed Sioux Indians, living in misery on their reservations, tormented by their loss of liberty, and mourning over the wanton destruction of the buffalo that had fed and clothed them, responded to the revelations of this new "medicine man" or "prophet" whose counsel might have been taken from the teaching of Christ. His message was a key that unlocked the vaults to their lost hopes and a door that gave them a glorious vision of the future. Every Indian on the reservation talked about it, and a surge of restlessness swept among them as they looked into the sky, hoping to see the Messiah coming—and their suppressed yearning to dance was revived. The chiefs feared trouble with the government unless the Indians were calmed down, and called a council to discuss what to do. They decided to send two of their members, Chiefs Kicking Bear and Short Bull, to interview Wovoka and learn if the report of his vision and the coming of the Messiah was truth or rumor.

The land of the Paiutes was a long way beyond the horizon. The two chiefs had never been that far from their home hunting grounds, and they would have to pass through the territory of other tribes that had never been friendly to the Sioux, but they set out without fear, encouraged by hopes that the vision of Wovoka was true. They traveled over mountains and across deserts for nearly 2,000 miles, munching the dried meat they carried, and picking wild fruit and berries to sustain their strength. At last, after a full moon had passed and come back, they reached their destination and found Wovoka in a wooden lodge near the lake. He received them cordially, and told them that many others had come to hear the words of truth the Great Spirit had given to him for the Indians. He said that the Messiah would appear soon, that he would drive vast herds of buffalo, wild horses, deer, and elk before him. He told them about the dance that had been enacted before him in his vision, and taught them the rites that accompanied it, then urged them to hasten back to their people, the Sioux, and convey to them the message of the Messiah's coming and instruct them in how to perform the dance.

Kicking Bear and Short Bull retraced their paths to the Pine Ridge Reservation, scarcely stopping to sleep. The people were restlessly awaiting their return and a general council was called. The prophet had convinced them that the Messiah was coming. Their reports of him and what he had said furnished the spiritual balm that the Indians needed and released emotions that had been seething within them like the lava in a volcano about to erupt.

They had not held a Sun Dance for a long time, for such ceremonies were prohibited on the reservation; but now, with the Messiah commanding them, they probed into storage boxes for discarded but cherished ceremonial costumes, and within a few weeks the light of campfires illuminated the spots where they danced in a frenzy of religious revival to the rhythmic beating of tom-toms.

Most of the government agents scattered in offices throughout the vast territory of the Sioux and Cheyenne had been at their posts long enough to know that the Indians had neither the potential nor the equipment to go on the warpath again. They were informed about the religious significance of the ceremonies and tolerated them, for they gave the Indians something to keep them occupied and lessened the minor disturbances that broke out between tribes and individuals. But when the newspapers in the East began printing stories of a strange "Ghost Dance" craze among the Indians, associated with mysticism and a belief that a Messiah was coming, officials in Washington became alerted although not disturbed. They did not become alarmed until R. F. Royer, a newly appointed agent at the Pine Ridge Reservation, wired the government that the Indians were on the "verge of a big outbreak" and that Sitting Bull was promoting it. Nothing could have aroused greater concern in the nation's capital, for the renowned medicine man was the most feared and unpredictable of all living Indians. He had returned from his self-imposed exile in Canada two years before and surrendered to the authorities at Fort Randall after being guaranteed immunity. He remained at the fort as a virtual prisoner until 1883, then was allowed to go to the Standing Rock Reservation. There is no official record connecting him directly with the Ghost Dance craze, but he was seen as a spectator at one dance, and that was enough to identify him as a leader if not a promoter of the movement.

The report from Royer, supported by newspaper accounts, incited the War Department to action, and General Miles, who headed the division of military affairs in the Indian Bureau, decided on a two-pronged action: first, to arrest Sitting Bull; and second, to disarm all the other Indians.

Some troops had been distributed throughout the Indian Territory, but immediately more were dispatched, including the old Seventh Cavalry. This was ultimately to prove a disaster that would leave an indelible stain on the pages of American history. Word that they were to be disarmed and their religious dance suppressed reached the Indians ahead of the new troops, and some of the tribes packed up and fled into the Bad Lands, where they could continue their ceremonies and survive by hunting and fishing for a short time until the Messiah came.

Weeks passed without any assurance from the Great Spirit; weakened by hunger, their enthusiasm dimmed, some of them went back to their reservations; others gave themselves up to the troops and were escorted back. On the remote areas of the reservation, however, many bands continued with their dances and hope still sustained them in their belief. Among these were the remnant of a tribe of about 400 men, women, and children headed by their hereditary chief, Big Foot, who was not as well known as Chief Red Cloud,

Sitting Bull, or Crazy Horse, but who was widely respected as an apostle of peace and who had, on occasion, exerted a calming influence when other bands were talking of going on the warpath.

From the accounts my father gave of him, Big Foot was of the type of old chiefs who came before the public prior to the end of the nineteenth century. He was comparatively free of revenge and believed that a lasting peace was possible between the Sioux and the Whites. He had not come to his high position by inheritance alone. In the days when he was growing up, a youth had to prove his worth before he was accepted as a leader of a tribe or band, and this was achieved through personal bravery, daring deeds in battle, swiftness on the chase, or by oratory and wisdom shown in council meetings.

My father said that Big Foot had less trouble in his band than did most other chiefs, because of his just rulings and unselfish motives. "He walked upright and often prayed to the Great Spirit for guidance," he said. "As a boy and youth, he passed the tests that showed he had the kind of mettle that entitled him to leadership. In addition, he was one of the best-known hunters among the Sioux."

Several years before the Ghost Dance trouble, Big Foot and a number of other chiefs were in Washington for a meeting with government officials. At that time I was working in the Indian Department. Even at that early date Big Foot could see the need for a mission school at or near the forks of the Cheyenne and Cherry rivers and recommended that one be established there. He agreed to sponsor the school and influence his band to send their children to it. However, at that time the government had no definite educational policy for the Indians and his suggestion was pigeonholed and forgotten. If this school could have been established and operated as a community center, the disaster at Wounded Knee Creek might never have occurred.

Like most of the leaders of the Sioux, Big Foot believed the Messiah was coming and permitted the members of his band to dance at will, but did not allow any disrespect toward the missionaries. Three churches—Catholic, Episcopal, and Congregational —had for many years maintained missionary schools there. Many of the Sioux children attended and learned the etiquette, customs, and arts of the White people. The missionaries were informed about the so-called new religion that was gaining such a large following among the Indians. They felt that it was a temporary phenomenon and soon would be recognized as religious folly by the aborigines, but it was frightening settlers and government employees who did not know the Sioux language or psychology and mistook the strange dances as an indication that an uprising was being planned. Some of the settlers left the area seeking refuge, and government employees stationed in outlying districts were brought into the agency offices, where they could have the protection of police and soldiers.

I must note here, as a memorandum of the disorganized state of affairs among the Indians, that there were quite a number who did not embrace the new religion or participate in the dances. In the fall of 1888 when the frenzy was reaching its peak, a large group of these dissenters made their camp close to the Holy Rosary Mission School about five miles from the Pine Ridge Agency. The sisters and priests investigated the camp and sent word to other schools and missionaries that there was no danger and to keep their schools open. However, the government boarding school at Pine Ridge was deserted by the students who left to join their parents in camps, and one of the buildings was burned.

Events began to reach a climax in the fall of 1890 when the government, for some unknown but apparently obtuse reason, failed to make the regular clothing issue to the Indians and cut their ration of beef to about one-half the usual amount.

CHAPTER VI

FLIGHT

As winter approached, Big Foot and his band were camped in a desolate wilderness five miles above the mouth of Cherry River near the Cheyenne. They were miserably armed with old shotguns and rifles suitable only for hunting small game. They were practically without rations, since they had received only a pittance of food in the fall issue at the agency. Their hunters were able to bring in a few rabbits and birds, which was little more than enough to feed the babies and young children, who were always taken care of first.

In the old days, before the government invaded their land and placed them on reservations, Big Foot had never let his band get into a perilous situation like this where they were hungry and scantily clothed. He would have selected a camp in a sheltered nook where wood, water, and game were plentiful. The Indian women would have dried meat, wild fruits, pemmican, Indian turnips, and other foods for their winter needs; and to these they would have added medicinal plants such as roots, shrubs, and leaves that experience had taught them to use in times of sickness. Their dried food would have been supplemented with fresh venison and other meat. Tepees and robes of buffalo fur and the skins of other animals would have been ready for the stinging north winds and the snows that were sure to come with winter. They would have piles of wood or buffalo chips ready to assure them of warmth and comfort even when subzero weather came.

The young would have been instructed in the customs and laws that governed the tribe, and religious dances and devotions to the Great Spirit would have been a part of the camp activity. But all these things belonged to a past that was far, far away as they hovered in their scraggly canvas tents on the banks of the Cheyenne that night, shivering from cold and tormented by hunger.

Several councils had been held in an effort to determine what they should do. They knew that the government troops were camped not many miles away. Red Cloud, the aging but respected chief, had sent an invitation for them to go to Pine Ridge Reservation, and they were debating this when a runner brought to them word that Sitting Bull had been killed.

A few hours later a group of Indians went to their camp from the Standing Rock Reservation and confirmed the report and gave more details of the murder—for that was what the Indians believed it to be, and what they believe today.

The great chief, who had risen to the highest pinnacle of prominence among the Indians through his wisdom and his unyielding defiance of the White man, had settled down in a camp on the Standing Rock Reservation. His close followers were there with him, and they were living peacefully. The group had accepted the new religion, but Sitting Bull had not taken an active part in it. He had never become reconciled to what had happened to his people, but he saw the uselessness of any further revolt and cautioned them to peacefulness.

General Miles arranged for the police at the Standing Rock Agency to arrest him on the grounds that he was inciting trouble through the dance and his support of the belief that the Messiah was coming. On the morning of December 15 he was awakened by a detail of Indian policemen from the agency, including Sergeants Red Tomahawk, Bull Head, and Shave Head. They found the chief asleep on the floor of his cabin and ordered him to get up and put his clothes on. He obeyed, but anger flashed in his eyes when they told him he was under arrest, which was an indignity that aroused all the fighting blood left in his nature. It was the first time a member of his race had put a hand on him except with affection, the deepest humiliation he had ever suffered. His voice rose in anger and protest as the officers seized him and marched him from the cabin with Bull Head and Shave Head holding his arms and Red Tomahawk behind him with a gun in his hand.

Some of his people heard the disturbance in Sitting Bull's cabin. The policemen who accompanied the sergeants were holding them back when one of them fired a shot which hit Bull Head. As he stumbled, he snatched the gun from the holster and shot Sitting Bull in the back. An instant later, Red Tomahawk fired another shot into Sitting Bull's back, and he pitched into a heap at their feet. Either bullet would have killed him instantly.

Immediately after receiving the detailed report, Big Foot called a council. They deliberated for two days, or until they heard that the government had assigned a detachment from Camp Bennett, on the Missouri River, to take them into custody. They also had a report that another group of soldiers was searching for them. This brought a quick decision. The council voted to start immediately for the Pine Ridge Reservation. It was the same spirit of freedom that had motivated the Pilgrims to leave Europe and cast their lot on the dangerous shores of a New World. Big Foot knew that the only chance they had to reach their destination was to get beyond the reach of the soldiers that night. He also knew that with his poor equipment he had no chance of success in battle with the soldiers. Early he had developed a horror of open warfare with the soldiers, and he preferred the old Indian custom of getting out of a difficult situation by stealthy movements in the darkness of the night.

The brightest side of the picture in taking his band to Pine Ridge was the fact that of the Sioux chieftains, Red Cloud had been most successful in dealing with the government. Through his influence, the objectionable army forts in their great Western hunting grounds had been removed, and many of his other plans had been approved.

The distance to Pine Ridge was more than 150 miles, yet Big Foot did not hesitate, for as a young man he had chased the buffalo and other wild game over the intervening country and had accurate knowledge of the streams, buttes, cut banks, and the Bad Lands over which they would travel. He had no compass, no maps, no roads, only dim trails and the stars to guide him. Though the ravages of old age had sapped much of his strength, he believed that it was the wish of the Great Spirit that he lead his band to a bloodless victory, to the Promised Land of Pine Ridge.

Without further consideration word was given for the band to break camp immediately. Although all the Indians knew of the great danger of being overtaken, the long march, their shortage of food and supplies, the possibility of a blizzard at that time of the year, and the many disagreeable phases of the trip, not a word of objection was raised, and not one Indian deserted; so in the quiet of the winter night, unseen and unheard by the two military camps, Chief Big Foot and his band were on their way to Pine Ridge. They silently trudged along, knowing that the military authorities would send soldiers to apprehend them if it became known that they were leaving the reservation. However the desire for justice and freedom burned in their breasts so strongly that they were undaunted by the pangs of hunger, or the biting blasts of the icy winds. Everyone, even the small children, knew that their safety depended upon swift but silent marching until they were out of danger. It was only natural that they had a strong feeling against the army, for it was responsible for their present danger and sufferings. They had fear that they would be captured or murdered as had other bands of Indians in the years past. They were indignant because they knew they had wronged no one and had been true to their treaty, but the government had not; yet it was the Indians, not the government people, who were suffering.

Unfortunately Chief Big Foot contracted pneumonia, but he kept at the head of the band as it was he who had to guide them aright. So great was his desire and determination to reach his destination safely that he gave no thought of his own danger, and believed in the justice of his actions so strongly that he felt that he had the guidance of the Great Spirit in this difficult task of rescuing his people from the clutches of the United States Army.

A few hours before daylight they came to a protected spot and at Big Foot's orders made camp. No light, no fire, no noise, and no food save scraps hurriedly gathered when they started, but they were soon asleep. The guards were watchful, and some of the most faithful were sent back a few miles to see if the soldiers were following them and had been instructed to immediately give the alarm. Fortunately, no dangers were encountered that night, which had been remarkably quiet. Only now and then a smothered cry from a hungry baby was heard, as the alert mother calmed it by putting it to her almost milkless breast.

As the stars began to fade, the sick chief sent his Dog Soldiers to awaken the camp with the instructions that they must again be on the march. The ponies had been picketed out in order that they might graze, as the Indians knew that their ability to get to their destination quickly depended largely upon the strength and endurance of their ponies; so they had been watered, and now were ready for the new forced march.

All day they marched, not stopping at noon, only occasionally for the ponies to rest; and Big Foot was still at the head of the band, guiding them accurately over hills and hollows, not daring to cause them to travel an extra mile as he knew of their suffering from hunger, cold, and anxiety.

The sun was fast sinking over the western hills when the chief, with the help of his faithful wife, stood up in the wagon and scanned the country to get his bearings, and at once recognized a good place where on a former occasion he had camped with a party of hunters.

There was wood and water, and by camping on

the south side of the little butte, they would be protected from the north wind. Fires were now permitted, the restraint of quietness was removed, and the Indians and their leaders felt that they would have a good night's rest. The ponies were again properly watered and driven a short distance to a place where the grass was good and where a valley protected them from the cold wind.

Chief Big Foot's contented moments were soon to be disturbed, as several women with their babies on their back in Indian fashion made their way to his tent and timidly but pathetically informed him that they were famished for lack of food, from exposure and travel, and that their breasts contained no milk, so that their babies were actually starving.

The tender-hearted and sympathetic chief bid them to come into his tent, where he gave them the last morsel of food he had. The situation now was deplorable, as the entire camp was out of food, but not wishing to add any more cares to the sick chief, he had not been informed of their starving condition.

Again his Dog Soldiers were instructed to make a detail of the best-known hunters in camp, and they were told to travel east, west, and south in quest of any kind of game that could be found; and in a remarkably short time the hunting party was on its way. They were supplied with all the weapons and ammunition they could muster. Among the hunters were four young men who were more adventurous than the others, and realizing that the men could not in the limited time allowed them find sufficient wild game for so many hungry people, they decided to take their riding ponies and travel in a northerly direction, where they had seen herds of cattle grazing on a distant hill.

After going over the first hill that hid their movements from the camp, they traveled due north. The wind was from that direction, and they could be reasonably sure that the cattle would drift south, so they soon deployed with the understanding that the hunter who sighted the cattle was to give the signal by imitating the yap of a coyote.

In a short time one of the Indians came upon the cattle bedded down in a coulee, or ravine. Retreating to the top of the hill, he gave the signal, and soon the four men were again together. They decided that since they had traveled to the north the pursuing soldiers might be camped within hearing of a gun shot, so it was decided that the lariat and the hunting knife must be the only weapons used. One of the four Indians was detailed to hold the saddle ponies in a clump of scrub timber near the unsuspecting cattle while the other three, one with a lariat and the other two with hunting knives, silently crawled over the hill toward the sleeping herd and stalked them as they often had stalked the buffalo, knowing that if the cattle stampeded there would be no beef for the starving band that night.

Keeping on the windward side and hidden by the tall prairie grass until they reached the proper distance from the cattle, the critical moment arrived for the hunters. The most skillful roper was given the important task of manipulating the lariat. Could he, from the difficult crouching position he must maintain, twirl the rope with dexterity sufficiently to place it over the horns of the large fat cow that had been selected as the victim? His steady nerve did not fail him, and his aim was accurate; the surprised and struggling critter was within their power while the remainder of the herd went thundering down the valley. The sound of the coyote yap from one of the Indians hurriedly brought the other Indians and the saddle ponies to the scene of the struggle.

With skill born of experience, the remainder of the task was accomplished within a short time, and soon the men were on the way to camp, each carrying a quarter of good beef. The other hunters came straggling in at about the same time with what they had been able to kill, which would have been totally inadequate to stay the hunger of so many ravenous appetites, but the beef fed the multitude. (The meat from jack rabbits, cottontail badgers, owls, and hawks was cooked, but saved for the nursing mothers and the children.)

Preparation of the meal was the work of the Indian women, and soon the meat was ready to distribute to the various families and groups of the other Indians. The Dog Soldiers were responsible for dividing the meat in proportion to the number in the family. Again, this is proof of the remarkable skill

[6 7]

of the Sioux, as they divided the food for the camp in a manner that all were satisfied.

As soon as the meal had been devoured, the Indians quickly and quietly went to their tents and slept. Chief Big Foot sent guards to the rear to be on the lookout for the soldiers, but again good fortune favored them, and no enemy was in sight.

The night was not so quiet as the starving and yelping dogs fought over the bones and leftovers, while the grey wolves, attracted by the smell of the meat, howled from the nearby hills.

Just before the last stars melted from the approaching sunrise, Big Foot awoke. Upon stepping from his tent he turned to the east, the west, the north, and the south, and gave thanks to the Great Spirit for the safety of his camp, and for the food procured the night before. He then caused the camp to be awakened and made ready for moving immediately.

The ponies had been brought in, but no breakfast was served to the Indians for the reason that all had been eaten the night before except for a liberal supply which was sent to the tent of Big Foot to save for the nursing mothers so that the babies were fed their breakfast with a bountiful supply.

Big Foot was restless to be on his way, as one of his chiefs, who had the reputation of foretelling the weather conditions, predicted that a blizzard would strike within three days. He based his prediction upon the three hoots of the owl at sundown. Big Foot and his chiefs knew that if a severe blizzard did come before they reached Pine Ridge, it would cause many deaths and much suffering among their people, so he led his band out of camp at a faster pace than on the preceding day.

The day's march was rather well defined and the territory was less rugged than that which they had passed through the two previous days. They believed the coming night would be the last time they would have to camp on the prairie, so their spirits were improved, and they urged their mounts and teams on and on. Occasionally, here and there a song could be heard as they encouraged each other through their misery.

Before darkness overtook them they reached the coveted place and camped on Medicine Creek, which was protected by hills and timber, and they felt that they were out of danger of being overtaken by the soldiers; so all was well, except for the fact that there wasn't any food. Big Foot realized that his men were too near exhaustion to be expected to go on another forced hunt, so he informed one of his chiefs to select a few of the yearling colts that still had some flesh on their ribs and to slaughter them for food. This was done, but with grief by the Indians, as the Sioux love their horses very dearly. Only the gnawing hunger and their weakness would cause them to eat the flesh of their horses.

Morning came, and after a brief devotion to the Great Spirit, the band again was on the march, hoping to reach Pine Ridge by night. There they knew they would be welcomed by Chief Red Cloud, and by their relatives, who would furnish them with food.

The forced march was continued with Chief Big Foot growing weaker, but still at the head of the procession. On and on they traveled over the dim trail that seemed never to end, but finally they came to what Big Foot recognized as the outskirts of the Pine Ridge Reservation, and he paused for a moment to give thanks to the Great Spirit; but the agency and safety were still several miles away. He prayed that they would be able to get there before the sun went down. They had not gone much farther when an ominous shadow appeared in the south. What could it be? Surely not the soldiers, for they would be coming from the north, but still the shadow approached.

"Soldiers," someone shouted. There could be no mistake, as the keen eyes of the Indians distinguished the well-known blue uniforms, the guns, the soldiers on horseback, and the mule teams.

By that time, Big Foot could hardly talk because of his weakness. However, with the help of his chiefs, he halted the caravan, and all were instructed to wave a white flag as a token that they came in peace.

Past events crowded into the chief's memory. He thought of the fate of Crazy Horse, Sitting Bull, and of the dishonorable deeds the Whites had committed against the Indians; but in these harrowing moments, the old chief remained firm in his determination to avoid a battle, and while some of his followers advised resistance, he instructed his band to keep the white flags flying so that the soldiers could see them at all times. His only thoughts now were for his people, and he was sad indeed. It was not until the soldiers were close and he was able to see their flag and its insignia that alarm struck into his mind, overpowering all his other thoughts and emotions. He was face to face with the Seventh Cavalry, the old Custer outfit that the Indians feared more than any other military force in the West. He had heard that they were in the field, and now he knew they had been assigned to the Pine Ridge Reservation, and he could understand their approach from the south. For a moment, as the enormity of the situation confronted him, he almost collapsed, and only by a superhuman effort was he able to save himself from falling. He called to those around him to keep the white flags flying and not to resist as the blue-clad enemy charged upon them as if immediate and total destruction were uppermost in their minds. Regardless of the warlike threat, not one Indian made a hostile movement, but all held the white flags in the air as the old chief had instructed them to do.

The Indians well knew from the actions of the soldiers that revenge was uppermost in their minds. The snappy commands of the officers were quickly obeyed, and they deployed as if to form the line of battle that the Indian warriors had seen on so many occasions. Even the machine guns were in place and ready to fire. Everything was prepared for action and the troopers were poised with their firearms when three officers, headed by Major Whiteside, approached the wagon where Chief Big Foot stood trembling from weakness, and demanded an immediate and unconditional surrender. He had expected the honor of a parlay during which he could explain where they were going, but quickly realized that it was not the time for even a discussion, much less an argument, so he agreed to the demand.

Through an interpreter, the Indians were given explicit instructions to march into the camp at Wounded Knee Creek, where the remainder of the army was stationed under the command of Colonel James W. Forsythe. Chief Big Foot waved a feeble arm with a forward motion, and the Indians moved on in the same direction they had been traveling; soon word reached those in the rear that they would be allowed to continue to the Pine Ridge Agency after camping overnight at Wounded Knee Creek. There was silent rejoicing among the few who had faith in the soldiers, but the chief had profound misgivings, and the sight of his gaunt warriors, half-starved children, bewildered mothers, and dependent aged, struggling with bowed heads and subdued expressions, hurt his pride and depressed his spirits. What was in store for them? Would they be murdered as was Sitting Bull and the great warrior Chief Crazy Horse? Would they be returned to the Cheyenne River Agency from which they had left and be mistreated as prisoners with all liberties taken from them? These and many other thoughts were tormenting his brain as his people silently obeyed the commands haughtily given by the soldiers. They had not figured out, as he had, why the soldiers had come from the south instead of the north as expected when they started on the march to Pine Ridge; nor could they understand why the soldiers should interfere with their rights to travel on their own lands. They were within the boundary of the Sioux Reservation, which was theirs by right of original ownership, and guaranteed in a treaty signed by Chief Red Cloud. But alas! They were in the hands of Custer's old command, the Seventh Cavalry of the United States Army.

Would this painful and silent march never end? The suffering from cold, hunger, and fatigue caused from the long march was now having its effect on all of the band, but to the aged, the nursing mothers, and small children, the fatigue was more than they could long endure. Even the leg-weary ponies and dogs moved forward with difficulty and hesitated; it appeared that the mental depression of the Indians had in some way affected these dumb animals.

The heart of the great chief was all but broken, as his mad dash for liberty had failed, and it was with humiliation that he accepted a comfortable tent which the commanding officer graciously offered to him. It was not of himself that he was thinking, but of his band who had trusted him to lead them to Chief Red Cloud's camp for protection. He thought of the council of Sioux chiefs awaiting his arrival to begin their discussion on the disputed question with the government. He knew of the importance of the council, and had definite ideas of how it might result in bettering his people's condition, if he could only get his band to Pine Ridge and offer his conciliatory plan. The confidence that he possessed in the Great Spirit had buoyed him to a point, but at the same time a strange feeling was engulfing him. Was it his physical condition that caused him to falter and to distrust the White people more than before? Was sickness and suffering robbing him of his facilities? He desperately fought to clear his mind of the fog that threatened to overpower him, as he realized that he was facing the greatest crisis of his long life, and he knew not what to do; so he prayed.

On that eventful night, the last night, Chief Big Foot's band was sleeping on a site selected by the soldiers whose guests, or prisoners, they were. They knew not which. A limited amount of rations had been issued to them by the commanding officer, and Chief Big Foot had been shown much courtesy, and had been given needed medical attention by the army physicians.

The next morning they were to break camp, hoping that they soon would join their friends and relatives at Pine Ridge. Their appetites had been partially appeased, and they had renewed hopes that in the morning they would be issued sufficient rations for their breakfast. Many of them, especially the women, thought they had been invited by the army officers to share the camp for the night and surely would not let their guests go away hungry. Therefore, it was but natural that the general gloom and the foreboding that had been their constant companion for many days and weeks would now subside, and that they would enjoy the blessings of a night of peaceful sleep. No longer did they fear that the soldiers from the Cheyenne River Reservation would overtake them and force them to return as prisoners. The fact that they were almost at the end of their journey stimulated the entire camp. Success was, they hoped and dared to believe, within their grasp. One more short march and they would, if floating rumors were true, be free to roam at will and live their own lives in their own way. This optimism was not shared by Chief Big Foot and his confidential chiefs, who well knew of the danger they were yet to pass through before being allowed to continue their journey to Pine Ridge.

One cloud had not been dispelled from the camp, as their beloved Chief Big Foot was yet suffering intensely, and they vainly wished for the service of their great medicine man Sitting Bull, whose skill they never doubted, and who was stilled in death by the hand of the race which was rendering medical attention to Big Foot. They, of course, had little faith in the White doctor, and who could blame them?

Now they had two camps within a few rods of each other, two races, two civilizations, two religions, two sets of moral codes, two sets of ideals, and two purposes in life, so let us take a view of the two peoples.

The soldiers' tents were lined up in military order; the cavalry horses, sleek and blanketed, munched their hay and oats in contentment while the big, rugged government mules, staked out with West Point precision, were biting and kicking each other in a playful mood. Supper had been served on time; cooking utensils and dishes had been disposed of in the usual military fashion. The officers' tents were pitched a short distance from and back of the enlisted men's; the tents' ropes were taut, and the canvas showed not a wrinkle, while inside the heat from the small stoves radiated comfort. All-wool government blankets piled high added to the prospect of a comfortable night for men who held the fate of the other camp in their hands. No doubt the officers, as well as the soldiers, were discussing the Indian situation, and perhaps enlarged upon the imaginary danger that they were in from the prostrate Chief Big Foot and his woebegone and disheveled followers.

"Custer's Massacre," as the White people called it, "revenge for annihilation of the old Seventh Cavalry," and other expressions were in common use, designed to instill hatred for the Sioux in the breast of the new recruits who had but recently arrived in the Indian country.

The Indian tents were rugged, patched, and dirty, pitched somewhat irregularly, and with but little uniformity, and the inside showed every sign of poverty. Robes, skins, and badly worn blankets had been thrown in the corner, while scant fire in the center of the tent filled it with smoke, but not much heat. Tired, sick, and crying children, lean and half-starved dogs, haggard and weary Indian ponies made up the Sioux camp.

Taps were sounded and the soldiers' camp became quiet, and all tent lights were extinguished; the Indians, out of respect for the military rule, became less noisy. The braves, after a visit to the chief's tent, had gathered in another tent to council on vital questions. They lowered their voices but continued to talk until late at night.

The ever-alert chief, too sick to meet with the council, had given instructions as to agreeing on plans about breaking camp, which would not be in violation of any of the rules of the soldiers. The Indian mothers returned to their own tents to make preparation for the night. Buffalo robes and blankets were placed for the various members of the family. Even the unusual conditions that existed on that last night did not prevent the mothers from arranging the beds of the various members of the family in accordance with the Sioux custom, in which the pallets, or beds, were assigned in order by age and sex.

The steady tramp of the guards who surrounded the camp, the keen click of the bayonets, and the sharp command of the officers could be heard in the stillness of the night when the guard was being changed. The Sioux must have marveled at all these maneuvers and wondered why all this precaution was necessary when there were no thoughts, at least on their part, of war or a surprise attack. The Indians were taking no such action, but they decided it was just another one of the foolish whims of the White race, and except for the customary horse wranglers their camp was unguarded.

The midnight hour had arrived, the swains had returned to their tents, and the lovelorn maidens drew their robes around themselves, ere sleep robbed them of consciousness, and thought of the young chiefs who on other and more suitable occasions and surroundings had played the love flute for their special entertainment. The grandmothers, ever alert for the safety of their children, especially for the marriageable daughters, were the last to seek rest. Years of experience and vigilance had taught them that they could not trust the White soldiers when the charms of a beautiful Indian maiden was the prize. These grandmothers had also learned from the experience of many winters that even the well-trained maidens from the best Indian families were not immune to the mating call.

Across the prairie the howl of the wolf was heard, and across the canyon its mate answered. Then the sulking coyotes took up the cry and made the night hideous by the wicked wail of the howling pack. The Indian mothers in Big Foot's camp, lying in their chilly tent, heard the howling and instinctively drew their sleeping infants nearer to them and cuddled them closely, fearing that harm might come to them, never dreaming that a far greater danger was much nearer than the wolves, and that on the morrow instead of the fangs of the wolf, the little bodies of their babies would be pierced by bullets from the guns of the soldiers of the United States Army, and that the mothers would be ruthlessly killed, and their unarmed warriors shot down like rabbits.

Big Foot, seriously ill, lay in an army tent suffering excruciating pain at every breath and thought of his faithful followers. Painfully he glanced at the east to see if there was any sign of the coming day. What would the new day bring? Would it be liberty and the blessings of friends and relatives, or would it be betrayal and death, as it had been to his long-faithful friend Sitting Bull?

The chief's wife had been awakened by his growing restlessness and knew from the chirps and calls of the birds that it was almost time for the light to appear in the east. She assured him that all was well with the camp, and urged him to sleep in order that he would be ready to head his band on the trip to the agency. For the first time during the night Big Foot slept.

The subchiefs rested but little during the night, as they feared for the life of Big Foot, who was growing weaker and his fever increasingly higher. They thought too of the safety of the camp, but would reassure themselves that they were under the protection of the friendly government. Did not the Treaty of 1868, which the chiefs knew by heart, say in Article One, "From this day forward all war between parties

[79]

of this agreement shall forever cease"? The government of the United States desired peace, and they pledged their honor to maintain it. Thus consoled, they too slept a little, not realizing that the Treaty of 1868 could be a mere scrap of paper.

The shrill notes of the bugle sounded reveille, and both camps were immediately astir; and the last night for Big Foot and his band was ended.

CHAPTER VII

THE MASSACRE

THE braying of the army mules and the fading stars indicated that a new day was drawing near, which gave Big Foot renewed hope that he might yet see his band safe with their friends at Pine Ridge, and that he would once more sit in the council with the mighty Sioux chiefs. It was in the councils that they deliberated upon new and important questions that meant so much to the Indian people, and if not wisely and satisfactorily adjusted, meant unhappiness, perhaps doom, for the great Sioux Nation.

The morning broke clear and cool. The mute hills that had witnessed so many tragedies in the animal world gave no warning that a human tragedy that would cause the profound sympathy of all Christian Americans was about to be enacted.

The wild animals and birds seemed to question the right of the unusual gathering, but they kept well back in the scattering pines of the nearby hills. The red, round sun appeared over the eastern horizon, and Big Foot thanked the Great Spirit for caring for them through the night, then reached out his hands in a mute appeal for deliverance from the army. He had spent a restless night, but by his strong will power had kept his mental facilities clear, though he was wracked with pain and exhausted from fever and exposure. He had a premonition that some evil was about to befall his band. He tried to have faith in the White people, but so many promises and failures on the part of the government caused him to have doubtful forebodings.

When the bugle sounded reveille, and the clear notes echoed and re-echoed through the hills, the Indians wondered if it was an ominous warning. Soon the camps were astir and anxious to finish the routine work. The Indians were eager to be on their way to Pine Ridge and, like their leader, were in great suspense, but the hope that they would be freed from the clutches of the United States Army sustained them. Surely if the soldiers had intended to do them harm they would have taken advantage of the darkness as they had done on other occasions; so they ate a scant meal and continued their preparations to break camp.

The soldiers under strict discipline had completed their morning details and duties with alacrity and were ready for the more serious work of the day. Just what was on their minds is today unknown, and history can never reveal it. Was it revenge for the Custer defeat on the Little Big Horn? Was the motto "Remember the Seventh Cavalry" embroiled in their minds, steeling them for a grim deed? Was an awful national crime being contemplated against the government's hungry and abused wards?

The army officers well knew that the Indians were at their mercy, and that a sure victory was theirs if they chose to make a kill. Can it be that an ambitious army officer, much like Custer, had a vision of military fame by wiping out this band of Indians camped within a stone's throw from his soldiers? Subsequently, events plainly indicate that some dark and subtle plot was hidden beneath the strange maneuvers. The slogan "The only good Indian is a dead Indian" was more often quoted then than now, and did much harm. Many Whites were prejudiced against them, and the slogan was used as propaganda to poison the minds of the soldiers who had just come to the Indian country to fight against an imaginary foe.

Hark, the commanding officer was sending out new orders! A hush, a quietness reigned for a moment. The orders were for the Sioux to approach the center and deposit all their arms at a designated spot. A signal from the sick chief caused the braves to obey the order, but alas, great insults were to be heaped upon them. Soldiers were ordered to search the tents, wagons, and bedrolls for arms. The women were searched and mistreated. All axes, crowbars, knives, and awls were taken from them and deposited with the guns. Helpless indeed were those worse-than-destitute Indians, as they could not kill or skin small game for their food, and could not erect or repair their tents. Such unreasonable demands had never before been enforced. Confusion and terror spread through the camp as soldiers rudely interfered with the women who were packing their camp utensils, but a gesture from the chief commanded silence.

Were these acts a deliberate effort on the part of the soldiers to provoke a quarrel? So it seemed to the Indians, but they were determined to remain true to their treaty and to the white flag of truce which they carried.

If Big Foot had had the remotest idea of fighting the soldiers, he would have done so when they first sighted the army near Porcupine Butte. There, he could have sent his warriors to the scattered buttes in the vicinity and made a creditable showing in the kind of warfare to which they were accustomed. Certainly such a plan would have sent Major Whiteside scurrying back for reinforcements, at which time the entire band could have slipped to the nearby Bad Lands, where pursuit would have been difficult, if not impossible. By that time, they knew that any show of resistance meant death to the band, as they were then wholly defenseless. What further demands could be made by the soldiers for an excuse to weaken their revenge?

The White man's history says that one of the Indians resisted being searched, and that during the scuffle his gun was discharged. Many of my friends who were survivors disputed that statement. They said no Indian had a gun, and there was no scuffle at that time by any of the Indians. It is reasonable to believe this, for after the firing of the gun, there was a general attack made on the Indians' camp. Even the Hotchkiss guns on the hill began firing. The simultaneous firing from all sources was strong proof that the soldiers were on the alert, ready to fire on a moment's notice; this included the infantry, the cavalry, and the Hotchkiss guns. Therefore, it appears that they anticipated trouble even if they had to start it themselves. It is difficult to conceive how the soldiers could imagine the Indians starting a fight under their well-known handicap. The army officials knew of the poor guns and the lack of ammunition in the hands of the Indians, as they had the chance to observe them the day before they marched into camp. Every word and act of the Indians was of peace and submission. Did they not immediately hoist a white flag after the soldiers were sighted, and did not their chief assure the army officers that he was a man of peace? Did they not keep a white flag flying continuously from the time they camped until it was shot down by the soldiers? Again, if the Indians had any intentions of fighting, surely they would have removed the women and children as they did at the Custer fight. Indians never subjected their families to the dangers of battle.

Thirty-five years ago James Mooney's wife gave me a copy of his report on the Wounded Knee Massacre, and the right to use it in any story. He was an unusually careful writer. In his report on the Massacre, which he sent to Washington, he stated:

"At the first volley the Hotchkiss guns were trained on the camp, and sent a storm of shells and bullets among women and children who had gathered in front of their tents.

"The guns poured in 2-pound explosive shells at the rate of nearly 50 per minute, mowing down everything alive.

"The terrible effect may be judged from the fact that one woman survivor, Blue Whirlwind, received fourteen wounds, while her two little children were lying dead beside her."

Within a few minutes 200 women and children and 90 Indian men were dead, and many others were writhing upon the ground. Among them was their chief Big Foot, who lay in a crumpled posture of death beside his shattered wagon. There were also 60 soldiers killed and others wounded by the cross fire of their own guns.

The tents of the Indians had been torn down by the shells, and some of them were burning above the helpless wounded; the surviving handful of Indians were fleeing in a wild panic to the shelter of ravines close by, pursued by scores of maddened soldiers and assaulted by firing from the Hotchkiss guns. There can be no conclusion except that the pursuit was a massacre, where fleeing women with infants on their backs, or in their arms, were shot down after resistance had ceased and almost every warrior was dead or dying.

The scene after the massacre was ghastly. Words

fail to depict the revolting sight: mothers wallowing in their own blood, or carrying lifeless infants, and leading or dragging bewildered children; fathers in the throes of death crawling around in a dazed condition endeavoring to find and unite their families; lovers wounded and in their dying moments whispering each other's names.

The dead soldiers were soon removed from the field by their comrades, and the wounded given medical attention, but not so with the wronged and suffering Indians. The soldiers were busy searching for hidden Indian women and children to kill instead of rendering relief to their fallen foe.

Three days after the massacre, when the last gun was fired and the search for survivors ended, the soldiers left, taking their wounded and captives to the agency headquarters on the Pine Ridge Reservation. Before darkness fell that night, a blizzard swept down from the mountains and smothered the battlefield in a white blanket, as if to blot out the bloody evidence of an unforgettable crime. In the shelter of the agency buildings, the soldiers had time to celebrate and gloat over their unholy victory, while their commanding officer prepared a report on how an assault by Indians on the warpath had been put down. Three days after the battle ended a detachment was sent to Wounded Knee to bury the Indians and bring in the wounded, if perchance there were any.

Anyone knowing of the severity of a South Dakota blizzard can hardly believe that the resistance of any human being would be sufficient to survive three days in a wounded condition while exposed to the fury of such a storm. Nevertheless the soldiers found a number of women and children alive, although badly wounded, or frozen, or both. Four babies were found under the snow, wrapped carefully in shawls by the dying mothers, who in their last moments thought of their loved ones and cuddled their babies close for protection and safety. Some wounded men were found several miles from the scene of the disaster. All the wounded were taken to the Episcopal Mission Church at Pine Ridge, which had been converted into a hospital to care for them. The Indian men who survived the tragedy were allowed to return to the battlefield to search for a lost child or wife. Too often, they had to stand beside the long trench that the soldiers had dug, and in voiceless pathos, watch as the soldiers dumped their loved ones, or a friend, into the trench. More than 200 bodies were dumped into that single grave that day. It seems that the spirit of revenge that motivated the Seventh Cavalry to destroy Big Foot and his band lingered on, as the soldiers buried their vanquished foe without ceremony or prayer. There were missionaries at Pine Ridge who would have been glad to conduct funeral services. The Reverend Father Craft, chaplain of the army at Wounded Knee, told me when I visited him in Stroudsburg, Pennsylvania, in 1924 that all the missionaries had received orders from Colonel Forsythe, who commanded the forces at Wounded Knee, that no mass or army burial would be given those "savages and Red devils," and that he stated, "Let them go to hell without a prayer."

General Nelson Miles, just before he died at Fitchburg, Massachusetts, told me that the Wounded Knee Massacre was a revenge for Custer. General Hugh L. Scott and Colonel Frank D. Bouldin told me the same story—that it was revenge for Custer and a claim of victory for whipping the Sioux.

Chief Big Foot often had said, "I stand for peace until my last day of life."

Many times I have been asked how the Indians feel today about the Wounded Knee Massacre, and my answer is that we do not believe the United States government would have allowed this to happen, or would have ordered the army to perpetrate it, if it had known the true facts of the condition of Big Foot and his band of 400 Indians who left their reservation to seek food at Pine Ridge and to be cared for by Chief Red Cloud.

CHAPTER VIII

FOOTNOTES
IN HISTORY

POWERFUL nations and empires have always been alike in one way: They brush the records of their mistakes and misdeeds under the rug, where they remain until the searchlight of history uncovers them. Even then, they are never more than footnotes in the records of the country where they occurred.

History is an encyclopedia of fables, folklore, and fiction. It is censored to sustain and maintain the ego of races, religion, and nations. It differs in every country. In Russia, communism is portrayed as a benevolent system of government, interested in the welfare of the common man. American history, as taught in school textbooks, pictures the development of a nation from the arrival of Columbus to the present in star-spangled language. Censorship has eliminated all malevolent and mischievous behavior from the pages of our past. The Indian is depicted as a savage and the White man as a good Samaritan. The honest story of the conquest of America is found only in the factual writings of researchers who have looked beyond the limited horizons of textbooks, encyclopedias, and government publications.

It has not been necessary for me to research into files to learn about the Wounded Knee Massacre. I was not present when it happened, but I was twenty years old and vitally concerned over what had happened. I knew some of the Indians who were slaughtered there, and I talked to the survivors. There were at least forty of them. Some of them went to Washington during the administration of President Franklin D. Roosevelt when a bill to recompense them was being debated in Congress. In a written appeal, they stated:

"The soldiers met at Porcupine Bluff. The Indians were flying the flag of truce, and the soldiers helped the sick Chief Big Foot stand in his wagon. The officers asked where he was going, and the chief replied that he was going to visit Chief Red Cloud at Pine Ridge. The officers ordered that he go instead to Wounded Knee Creek where they had their main camp, and the chief gave orders to his band to go in peace with the soldiers, which they did while still flying the flag of truce until it was shot down by the soldiers. When they arrived at camp, the soldiers brought food to them, they pitched their tents, cooked their food and ate. The soldiers took Big Foot to the

White man's doctor and gave him White man medicine. The subchiefs called a council and told all that Big Foot wanted to obey the officers of the army.

"The next morning the Indians were told to take their weapons to the center of the camp, which they did, leaving them on the ground. The soldiers searched the wagons and tents, searched the women, took axes, crowbars, awls, knives and everything they had. They brought Big Foot from the White man's tent where he was in conference, then ordered all the Indians to the center of the camp. The men sat on the ground, the women sat behind the men, and the soldiers surrounded the camp. A shot was fired, but the Indians had no guns and could not fire back. Then the bullets came like hail from the White man's guns. Many were killed, many ran to safety, and many soldiers were killed or wounded by their own guns. Wounded soldiers were carried away, but the wounded Indians were left to die."

Buried in the files of the Indian Bureau is a report of the information presented to Congress by interested witnesses after Representative Francis Case of South Dakota had introduced a bill to compensate the survivors of the Massacre. Those who are interested may obtain the report as I did. The following paragraphs from the report are quoted:

"The Wounded Knee incident properly has been called a Massacre. The historical facts are here set down as basis for judgment by Congress:

"The unrest and distress among the Sioux bands

had increased through a number of years prior to 1890. The cause of the Sioux misery need not be recapitulated.

"There have been ruthless violations of treaties and agreements, and numerous administrative abuses. It was hardly possible for the Indians themselves to know what spot they were permitted to inhabit and what they were forbidden to inhabit, so sweeping, and so casual had been the violations and unilateral abrogations of contract on the part of the Government.

"It is important to note that these Messianic revivals had taken place from time to time for many years among other Indian tribes, and in no instance had they thrown the Indians into aggressive warfare with the Whites. Neither acts of war, nor massacres, nor depredation had resulted from the numerous Messianic revivals."

Major James McLaughlin, who had been agent at the Standing Rock Reservation since it was established, reported that "The army was in complete possession of the field at the time, hence the government must be held responsible for the loot which followed the Massacre."

James Red Cloud, hereditary chief and grandson of the renowned Chief Red Cloud, was in Washington at the time the Committee on Indian Affairs was considering the Wounded Knee bill and was invited to testify. He said in part:

"In compliance with the orders of the United States government and the army, when they made these treaties with us we laid down our arms. At one time we held the entire country which you now hold. Although these treaties were made prior to that killing, you came in and murdered our babies. Through the treaty you made a pledge that anybody who committed an offense should pay the penalty for the survivors of the Wounded Knee Massacre."

Testimony from the joint report of Major J. F. Kent and Captain Frank D. Baldwin, following an investigation, furnishes proof that the Indians were correct in that the soldiers were killed or wounded by their own bullets at Wounded Knee. Here is a paragraph from their report:

"It is only natural that an army of men with revenge in their hearts would make such an error, but to blame it on the Indians is an old trick of the White people. For the unmilitary-like behavior of the soldiers and the lack of properly placing them, the commanding officer, Colonel James W. Forsythe, was court-martialed, and for a time was deprived of his command. The fact that he was accused by his superior officers is sufficient evidence to prove that the whole affair was irregular, and the stamp of disapproval was placed on his actions."

More revealing and conclusive than anything else presented at the hearing was a statement taken from the records of General Miles:

"In my opinion the least the government can do is to make a suitable recompense to the survivors for the great injustice which was done to them, and the serious loss of their relatives and property.

"The action of the commanding officer, in my opinion, was most reprehensible. The disposition of the troops was such that in firing upon warriors, they fired directly toward their own lines and into the camp of the women and children, and I have regarded the whole affair as most unjustifiable and worthy of the severest condemnation."

The bill never broke through the staunch, patriotic barriers in Congress. Its passage would have been an admission that the nation had been guilty of a crime. The government, no doubt, would have provided relief to the survivors of the Wounded Knee Massacre had they been hungry or in need; but it could not admit that an offense had been committed against their people a half-century before. This would have shattered the traditions that hold the nation above reproach.

CHAPTER IX

THROUGH THE
MAGIC DOOR

THREE months after the Custer battle, I was sent to a boarding school the government had started on the Sioux Reservation. It was 200 miles from our village of tepees to the big, unpainted schoolhouse and dormitories and a white church with a steeple that pointed to the residence of the God we were to learn about.

More than 200 children were assembled there. I was six years and three months old. I do not know how I got there, but I remember the sadness I felt when I left my parents and the fear that came when I first saw those stern buildings. I entered them with terror in my heart, for about all I knew of the White man was that he was a fierce warrior who was killing our buffalo and taking over our land. Although almost everything is vague in my mind, I remember a woman teacher who had learned our language and understood the emotions we were suffering in a completely foreign environment.

I remember attending church and being told about the Christian God. He was an impressive being, like the Great Spirit of the Sioux people. I liked the music and hymns, and the costumes of the priests and nuns. It was in their church that I knelt on my knees for the first time. I stared at the bare floor, and as time passed, I learned to close my eyes and listen to the prayers. I had been taught that the Great Spirit was everywhere and that the water in the pools of the Black Hills was his tears. This God lived in a place called Heaven. He had many angels. There also was a place called Hell where the Devil lived, and he wanted to get me into his kingdom even at that age.

I will have to skip over much of what happened during the four years I spent there. I studied English and soon learned enough to understand the meaning of the word "savage," and to know that it applied to the Indians. One day I became brave enough to ask the woman teacher why the Indians were called savages. She looked at me thoughtfully, and with what I can now see was compassion, and her answer was the first glimpse I had of myself as an individual. It opened the doorway into problems and difficulties that awaited me in adjusting to the conditions and demands of a new civilization. Until then, my feelings

[97]

were a mixture of regrets for the past and hostility toward the future. It was much deeper than the resentment the growing-up generation feels today for what they call the "establishment."

I will repeat in essence what the teacher told me in that far distant past:

"When you came here, Red Fox, your mind was untrained and unstained in the ways of the White man's living. Before you leave here, you will have learned that there are good and bad people in all races. Do not listen to those who call the Indian a savage. They do not know American history and they are not good Christians, because a good Christian does not condemn his fellow man."

When I entered the school I had no thought but that I would spend my life in a tepee and hunt buffalo as my father had. Even by the time I was ready to leave, I had no more than a vague idea of what lay ahead for me, but a magic door had been opened that would take me from the ABC's to calculus; from a tepee lighted with buffalo oil burning in a clay dish to the electric lights in a penthouse; from messages sent through puffs of smoke made by a blanket over a campfire to a swift interchange by telephone; from the horse to the superjet; and lastly, perhaps more significantly, from the arrow to the hydrogen bomb.

Had I been told in prophecy that I would meet the people who carved these advances out of dreams and imagination, I would have had no comprehension of what was said; but when I finally met them and moved along with their "progress," I wondered if my elation compared to that of the White man; or did my heritage and lingering love of the past lessen my appreciation for the achievements of another race and the personalities it produced?

I met Thomas Edison and Alexander Graham Bell, and many others who impressed me as great people, but pride in them and their achievements has not overawed me, for I am not convinced that the comforts and advancements which they brought into the world have made people more content and happy than the Indians were through the centuries on the mountains, prairies, and deserts of the primeval, virgin continent.

Adaptation to the ways of modern civilization was natural for me. I sort of glided into it. I have lived a storybook life and am not ungrateful for what the White man has given me, but the ghosts of my ancestors stalk me at times in the dark and congregate around me when I meditate in solitude. Although I have adapted to my environment, like immigrants have done, I am still a native of the wilderness. I did not come to this country in search of riches and freedom. I am as much a part of this country as the insensate rock and the Sequoia tree, as my ancestors were millenniums before me. I would be insensitive if I did not sorrow for the members of my race who are restricted still to the confines of a staked-out reservation

—still in the captivity of a foreign civilization. But my transformation was gradual. I had been four years in boarding school before returning to my home in the village, and it was a real joy to get back into my parents' tepee, wear moccasins again, and let my hair grow. That was in the month of May, 1878. My uncle, Crazy Horse, had been killed the year before, and I wept when my parents told me how a soldier had thrust a bayonet into his back, and when they quoted the words he spoke when he died: "I was hostile to the White man—we tried to escape, but the government would not let me alone. I came back to the Red Cloud Agency, yet I was not allowed to remain quiet. I was tired of fighting. I have spoken. . . ."

During that summer I reverted to the old Indian ways, but I became restless, for I had absorbed enough of the White man's knowledge to make me want more. In the fall I was sent to the Carlisle Indian School in Pennsylvania. On the night before I left I slept in a tepee for the last time. I was on the way to complete acceptance of the new civilization and the political, religious, and economic doctrines that made it a complicated system.

A few other Sioux youngsters accompanied me on a wagon ride to Kansas City, where we boarded a train—the first one I had ever seen. The ride was harrowing, for some of the passengers looked upon us as wild beasts that should be in a zoo.

I remember little of my first days at Carlisle except that I was given new clothing and shoes that hurt my feet. They had become accustomed to the softness and comfort of moccasins. One of the things I remember clearly is that boys and girls from many tribes were there. Many of them did not know English, but knew only their tribal language. Most of them, however, had learned the sign language, and I had fun talking to them and refreshing my knowledge of this universal medium of communication.

I learned a lot from books and teachers during the nine years I spent there, and I became acutely aware of who I was and curious about where I came from. These two questions were the main focus of my attention during those years that I was shaking off the clinging vines of the wilderness and taking on the finery of the culture that had adopted me and was trying to make me conform to its patterns of conduct and survival.

I remember discussions in class and in our rooms about where the Indian came from, and I remember asking why it was necessary to think he came from any other continent. "Where," I asked, "did the Japanese or Chinese, or the black people from Africa come from?"

No one could answer this question any more than they now can. Nothing new has been learned about this enigma during the 100 years of my life or, for that matter, for 5,000 years.

The Indians were spread from the Arctic to the

tip of South America when the White man came, and there was not a single member of any other race among them. They differed as much in their customs as the people of Europe or Asia.

The Eskimos who live in the land that is perpetually smothered in snow and ice have managed to survive and have excellent health without ever tasting fruit or vegetables. Nothing grows—not even a tree or blade of grass within hundreds of miles of them. How have they continued to live without the vitamins and minerals that the White man gets from oranges and molasses, or from drug store bottles and boxes? The answer is simple. When they kill a seal or catch a fish, they eat every part of it except the skin or scales. In this way, they obtain the minerals and vitamins and all other essential elements they need. They never have to process, refrigerate, or add preservatives to their food. In both North and South America, the Indians eat many kinds of wild fruit and berries and grow crops which give them substances their bodies need.

Where we came from is really a philosophical question, but archaeologists, theologists, ethnologists, and philologists have been investigating it for thousands of years. They still do not know where anyone came from, but have developed evidence that man has inhabited this ball of mud and water for a hundred thousand years, perhaps a million or more.

The White man's theories of where the Indian

came from are a hodgepodge of speculations, but all are formed from the premise that he is an offshoot of some other race. I remember one teacher reading from a Smithsonian publication that America was uninhabited until explorers from Asia came here over the Aleutian Islands that form stepping stones between the two continents. It is just as easy to believe that the Indians crossed over there and settled Asia, since whatever happened is less than an echo from the remoteness of time.

This presumption reflects the inborn arrogance of the White man, who believes that he is the first symphonic art work of God, and that if other races were created, it was afterthought—or that the Creator was weary or having a nightmare.

There are some ethnologists who believe that the races of man should be limited to three primary divisions—white, yellow, and black. They would put the Red man in the Mongolian cradle. As a matter of visibility, these specialists are color blind, for the Indians vary in complexion from light brown to near black. They have brown, black, and sometimes blue eyes.

The concept of an Indian as a huge, savage-looking primate with high cheekbones and wearing feathered headgear and a jacket decorated with squirrel tails is less true than the language definition of a member of the Caucasian race as White. The complexion of the "White" race goes through the spectrum all the way from dark, dark brown to saffron.

The Japanese, Chinese, and other so-called yellow races vary less, yet show up sometimes with blue eyes and sandy-colored curls. All kinds of people blush at times for their sins, giving them unity in one respect.

Even the least-informed ethnologists know that people living under the burning tropical sun for generations grow darker as the genes adapt the skin for protection. Similarly, those in the deserts become narrow-eyed from constant squinting in the sun's glare. High cheekbones are found only among a limited number of Indian tribes. Why, I do not pretend to know, unless perceptive nature was preparing them for appearances on television.

Discussions of where people came from were common before Plato ruled the intellectual colony in Athens. I remember talking about this with some adult Indians who came to Carlisle and heard a lecture by a teacher. One of the older Indians asked me if I could get a map of the world for him. I took one from the wall in a classroom and handed it to him. He asked for a pair of scissors, which I gave to him after being assured no teacher was in sight. He looked me in the face and said, "I have never been to school like the White men or you, but I will show you the way we came."

He cut the map until it was like a jig-saw puzzle, then glanced up and explained, "Many moons ago this land was all one big piece. The Great Creator came and washed some of it away, leaving water in its place. That is the way we came. Our people stayed where we are now."

He took the sections of South Africa and America and put them together, and explained, "Big water come, land move. New land come out of the water."

He pointed to the region of the South Atlantic Ocean between the two continents saying, "Maybe land here disappeared." He had either dreamed or heard about the continent of Atlantis that Plato told about and many others have speculated about, for again, he said: "Maybe that is the way we came."

He may have been right! Who knows? He was expressing a legend of a flood that is found in the folklore of all Indian tribes.

Some students have been puzzled by the difference in the cultural development of Indians in South, Central, and North America. At the time of Columbus the Aztecs, Mayas, and Incas had progressed in the arts and sciences to a level comparable with that which prevailed in Asia. They had achieved excellence in government; their people were prosperous, peaceful, and contented. They had learned the arts of weaving cloth and making pottery, and their engineers had built mountain roads that are still in use today. They cultivated crops for food, mined precious metals and learned how to smelt them, and made innumerable decorative, religious, and utilitarian articles from them. Excavation of ruins in Indo-China have brought up artifacts of long-forgotten cultures similar to those found in South America. The climate and environment between these two sections of the world are similar, and there is some evidence that the American Indian may have come across the Pacific Ocean, or he may have migrated and planted his primitive culture there. Who can say that in the dim past a vast archipelago or mid-Pacific continent may not have existed and been swept away by a flood? At least, this is as believable as the prevailing theory about Atlantis.

There are many other ideas about the origin of the Indians. The Mormon Church has formed the opinion from a verse in the Bible which states that "Over the earth your sons shall spread. Some will go east, some to the south and others to the land like the wings of a bird." A look at the world map will show that North and South America at least vaguely resemble wings of a bird.

There is another religious claim that the Indian race developed from one of the lost tribes of Israel. After reading these many theories, I am inclined to think that the old Indian with his world map was as close to truth as anyone. His illustration conforms to the belief of his people that when the Great Spirit created the earth, He created man on all the land.

In a test at Carlisle, I was asked how the Indian benefited after the Pilgrims landed. I was still quite young when I answered this, and as I remember, I mentioned only the good; there were some benefits like sleeping in a bed in a fine building and having my food served on a table. After all, I was not familiar with less auspicious benefits at that time, for I was unschooled in history, unversed in philosophy, and untrained in philology.

CHAPTER X

WITH

BUFFALO BILL

I THINK back upon the years I spent at Carlisle with a great deal of satisfaction. What I learned from books and teachers and the discussions we had prepared me for adventures and emergencies that were coming, although not programmed, in my life. From books I learned specific knowledge. Teachers tried to provoke my sluggish mental molecules into thinking, and the discussions gave me opinions about everything that had happened, was happening, or was likely to happen in the world.

During the summer months of my last four years at Carlisle, I became a sailor on the high seas. This started in the spring of 1884 when I was fourteen years old. Captain Charles Richard Pratt, the superintendent at Carlisle, summoned me to his office one morning and introduced me to a sea captain named

McCloud, who was master of a barkentine, the *Jose-phine*. He asked me if I had ever seen a sailing ship. I told him I had seen only pictures of them.

"Would you like to sail with me?" he asked.

I told him I would if Captain Pratt would let me.

The next few days I waited with excitement and neglected my studies. I had worked on a farm the previous two summers and enjoyed it, but the thrill of going out to sea in a big sailing boat and visiting strange places left my imagination stuttering on the doorsteps of a new and intriguing adventure. I had come to respect and admire Captain Pratt. I think most of the boys and girls there had a father image of him. We were far from our childhood homes and needed the understanding and affection of an older person. He was aware of this need and treated us with sternness when we needed discipline, and affection when loneliness for our homes on the prairies and hills was expressed in our voices and sometimes in our tears.

I began to tremble when he called me out of class before a week had passed. I made my way to his office and stood before him with hope and expectation in my face.

"Red Fox," he said, "I am sending you to Baltimore the day after tomorrow. Captain McCloud is signing you on as a cabin boy. Your salary will be three dollars a month."

He gave me $25 to buy rubber boots, a southwester, and other articles I would need on the voyage. I felt his eyes upon my back as I left his office, and the warmth of his smile was like a blessing.

My eyes were wide with wonder as I looked upon the sea for the first time. It was like viewing eternity in motion. The waves were rippling the waters of the Chesapeake Bay, and the sun was sinking into the embers of a campfire it had built along the horizon. The *Josephine* was tied to a dock and I went aboard with the emotions that Jason must have felt when he started upon his journey to find the Golden Fleece. I asked for Captain McCloud, but a sailor told me he was ashore, and took me to the crew's quarters. Only a few men were aboard, and I spent the next two hours wandering over the ship and staring into the water that caressed its sides as if each wave were in love with it.

I could scarcely contain my emotions as we were towed across the bay to Cape Charles and released to the caprice of the wind and the sea. The big sails were hoisted and billowed in the wind, and we began our southward journey at 12 or 14 knots an hour.

I waited on tables, helped the cook, and ran errands for Captain McCloud as the ship continued to plow through the waves day after day. I scanned the eerie heavens at night when dark clouds hovered or the stars sparkled in the sky and showed their faces in the sea. On the twenty-eighth day we sighted Sugar Loaf Mountain not far from the harbor of Rio de Janeiro. We spent four days there unloading our cargo of merchandise and taking on hundreds of sacks of coffee.

I learned something about seamanship on that trip, and during the next three summers I sailed on other ships that took us into ports from Maine to the West Indies.

By the time I finished my schooling at Carlisle, I had some knowledge about people in most of the world. I had studied the history of the United States, Europe and Asia, and I searched for information about the Indian tribes of America. There was no history about them before the time of Columbus except what had been preserved in folklore and memory. History books of today portray them as pagans and savages whose culture found its highest expression in rug weaving and in pottery making.

When I returned to my home and saw my parents for the first time in nine years, I realized that I had found a different world than that of the reservation Indians. My parents were living in a tiny house and wearing government-issued clothing, but the moderation of their environment had not changed their beliefs. They were saddened by what had happened to their people, which was reflected in the dejection of almost everyone I met. They had no desire to change and be like the White conquerors, and so were destined to carry their grief to their graves.

Their one solace was that their children could attend the White man's school. They visualized this as a way to escape the captivity of a reservation and be able to compete with the White man in his strange world.

I could see in my mother's eyes, when she was cooking over a wood stove, a desire to go outdoors and roast a strip of buffalo meat in an open fire; and in my father's expression as he studied me in my store-bought suit and necktie an urge to shake his head in disbelief at what he saw. I gave him an Ingersoll watch as a present, but realized that he would never regard it as anything but a trinket, for the sun had become a dial in his brain and it would continue to be his time-clock to the end of his days—just as he would judge the hours of night by the position of the stars in the sky.

My mother was pleased that I had brought her a dress, for by that gift she knew that I loved her and was still a dutiful son, but she fingered the strange fabric remembering the homespun, unbeautiful clothing of their freedom years. The swift changes that had come in their lifetime were enmeshed in the gossamer threads of memory—memory of the unmonotonous days when they roamed the wild terrain and pitted their lives against the whims of Nature.

I had been home but a few days when Major James McLaughlin, agent at the Standing Rock Reservation at Fort Yates, employed me as an interpreter, and after a few months sent me to Washington to serve in the same capacity for the Bureau of Indian Affairs. But nothing significant or memorable happened during the two years I was there, and so I re-

turned to Pine Ridge in 1893. It was then that I was
suddenly lifted up into the clouds of a fantastic
adventure that was to carry me over much of the world
and into the presence of people who were merchan-
dising its culture. They were dreaming of the automo-
bile, of the electric light and the telephone, plus
innumerable other advancements that would leave a
gulf comparable to 2,000 years of previous time between the nineteenth and twentieth centuries.

The pathway to adventure opened for me when
Colonel William Frederick Cody, better known as
Buffalo Bill, came to the Pine Ridge Reservation to
recruit Indians for his Wild West Show, which was
appearing at the World's Fair in Chicago. He talked
to my father and mother, then asked me to join his
show as an interpreter and have charge of the Indians.
I told him I was only twenty-three years old and
thought some of the older Indians would object to my
having charge of them. He disagreed with me, so we
went out to talk to some of the others about joining the
show and having me in charge. Their general opinion
was that "Red Fox knows the White people. He has
been to school."

One hundred and twenty signed up and were on
the way to a new life. They were the first group ever
rounded up for "show business," and many of them
were destined to stay in it and branch out individually
into vaudeville, the circus, and the movies.

We left Rushville, Nebraska, for Chicago on the
Burlington Railroad. Many of the Indians had never

seen a train, much less ridden on one, but this was a mild preliminary to what was coming as they reached their destination and saw the great city and appeared on the stage before thousands of people. They proved to be a successful innovation for Buffalo Bill. Crowds flocked to see them perform. Under the direction of a clever stage manager, they did rope tricks, held up stage coaches, did their tribal dances, and imitated the calls of animals and birds. Generally, their part in the show was built around ideas Americans entertained about the Indian and his primitive ways of life.

All that summer we played in Chicago, and I spent my free time visiting scenic places in the city, wandering among the crowds at the fair, strolling along the waterfront, and reading at the public library. There wasn't anything in books or magazines about the West as it is known today. Everything I read was of a serious nature, with the Indian still a troublesome problem for the nation. There was no romance, joy, or entertainment in the stories and articles. The section of the United States west of the Mississippi River was still being conquered by soldiers and developed by industry and agriculture, while the Indian tribes were struggling to maintain their ancient hunting grounds and to preserve what was left of their tribal rituals and customs. Outbreaks were infrequent, for the majority of the native Americans had been placed on reservations.

This situation was to change somewhat during my years in show business. Buffalo Bill was to have

Chief Red Fox.

Jack London, author and adventurer, San Francisco, 1904.

Teddy Roosevelt, Wyoming Territory, 1881. *(Inset)* President Theodore Roosevelt, steel engraving, 1904.

General George Armstrong Custer.

Cemetery Site, Battle of Little Big Horn.

COL. W. F. CODY

I AM CO

Lithograph poster for Buffalo Bill Cody's Wild West
Show, 1900. *(At right)* Advance card and poster, Cody's
Wild West Show, 1895. *(Far right)* Group photo,
William F. Cody and his Wild West Show company.

Indian chiefs and U.S. officials (Buffalo Bill Cody, standing, right center) at Pine Ridge, South Dakota, January 16, 1891.

Yellow Hand, Cheyenne Chief, killed by Cody in gun
duel at War Bonnet Creek, Wyoming, 1887.

FRANK F. CURRIER, PHOTOGRAPHER.

SITTING BULL, SWIFT BEAR, SPOTTED TAIL.
Ta-tou-ka-yot-la, Ma-to-o-ka, Sin-to-ga-li-ka,
Mi-nn-kon-you Chief. Ar-ap-a-ho Chief. Broule Chief.

JULIUS MEYER, RED CLOUD.

Studio photo, Sioux chiefs.
(At right) Sitting Bull, Sioux
chief, circa 1889.

Sitting Bull. Bismarck, Dakota Territory, 1885.

(Top) Chief Red Cloud, Oglala Sioux.
(Bottom) Chief Rain-in-the-Face, Sioux, circa 1885.

(Top) Chief Gall, Sioux, circa 1886.
(Bottom) Chief John Grass, Sioux. Line engraving, 1890.

Geronimo, Apache chief (mounted, at left); Natches, son of Geronimo, standing by his side. Circa 1886.

Geronimo, war chief of the Chiricahuas, Apache tribe.

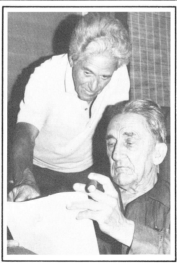

(Top) Chief Red Fox at Camp Double Lake,
Sam Houston National Forest, 1938.*(Bottom)* Red Fox
(with cigar) and editor Cash Asher.

an important influence in the transition. Many "Wild West" magazines would spring up, movie makers would feature the Red man in their pictures, and fiction writers would concoct innumerable weird and sinister stories about them, with "heap big" imagination added. Gradually the one-time savage was to become a flamboyant, colorful figure. Will Rogers, Vice-President Curtis, and Senator Owen, who were of part-Indian blood, were entering the limelight, giving the whole Indian race a dignity and prominence that was far removed from the old frontier days. People began boasting that they had Indian blood in their veins. It was not something to hide in their ancestral closets.

In his attitudes and beliefs, Colonel Cody was close to being a full-blooded Indian. His treatment of those in the show was always kind and understanding, and his voice was often raised in defense of them in Washington. Often he talked in our tent over a cup of coffee. He told me of his life on the frontier as a boy of sixteen when he was a Pony Express rider. He was born in Scott County, Iowa, in 1846, but drifted west when he was fifteen years old. He served as a Union scout during the War Between the States, and while the Kansas Pacific Railroad was being built across the prairies, he killed buffalo to supply meat for the workers.

The man who had much to do with making him famous and promoting his show was a writer named Ned Buntline, who was dramatizing the West in his stories and bringing the Indian into perspective with perception and sympathy. He had written a manuscript showing Buffalo Bill killing Indians while he was with the Pony Express, and asked his approval before publishing it. He offered Buffalo Bill $200 for this right.

"Red Fox, were you ever afraid of yourself?" he asked me.

"No," I replied.

"After reading the story I was afraid of myself —killing three Indians with two shots. Frank Butler or his wife Annie Oakley could not have done that well, could they?"

I asked him if he accepted the $200.

"Yes," he said, "and Buntline agreed to send me that much every month if he sold the stories he planned to write." The stories Buntline wrote helped to bring Buffalo Bill into prominence as a dashing, glamorous figue as the West was being industrialized and "civilized."

Cody told me that the stories about his duel with Chief Yellow Hand were inaccurate. It had been reported that they fought with knives. This is how Cody explained what happened:

It started when General George Crook sent for Cody to do some scouting after a band of Cheyennes had left their reservation, headed for Canada. Their intention was to join the northern Cheyennes and Sioux who had fled after the battle with Custer. One day a Cheyenne warrior rode into General Crook's camp under the flag of truce and through an interpreter told the general that his chief wanted to fight Buffalo Bill. He said that if the chief killed the scout he was to let the Cheyennes go to Canada, but if the scout killed the chief, they would return to their reservation in peace.

General Crook contacted Buffalo Bill, who agreed to the duel even though Chief Yellow Hand was his friend. If he rejected the challenge, the military officers and men, and the Indians as well, would call him a coward, so he was forced into the duel.

The Cheyenne warrior waited at the camp until he heard that Buffalo Bill had accepted the challenge, then rode away. Two days later, he returned and told the general that his chief would be ready to fight the duel the next day at high sun, which was midday.

At War Bonnet Creek in Wyoming, in the month of August, 1887, the officers, men and scouts lined up with a flag of truce flying. As Yellow Hand and his band rode in, they also carried a white flag for peace. Yellow Hand threw the cue stick upon the ground, which meant he was ready. Buffalo Bill threw his hat upon the ground to show that he was ready. They rode out and circled each other as fast as their horses could run. Yellow Hand fired the first shot. The bullet hit the horn of Buffalo Bill's saddle. He fired then and killed Yellow Hand's horse. Yellow Hand dropped to the ground. Buffalo Bill dismounted, and Yellow Hand fired again, but missed. Buffalo Bill fired again, hitting Yellow Hand in the throat, and he died almost instantly. Buffalo Bill had not wanted to kill him. This scene has been reproduced on the screen and television, but pictures the two men fighting with knives.

After the show closed that first year and went into winter quarters at the fair grounds at Trenton, New Jersey, I spent my time in libraries, sight-seeing and visiting historical places, and associating with Indians wherever I could find them.

CHAPTER XI

GERONIMO'S REVENGE

IN 1894 the show opened at Brighton Beach, New York, and we played there all season to large crowds. Not much of importance happened, but the next year Buffalo Bill put his show on a train and we toured the heartlands and big cities of the United States and Canada.

I loved the excitement of travel, but my enthusiasm collapsed sometimes as our train rolled over farmland and through small towns in Oklahoma, Nebraska, Iowa, and other midwestern states where the wilderness had been untouched and the Indians had lived in the unspoiled splendor of nature not many years before. Members of many different tribes came to see the show when we were near their reservations. I always managed to talk to them about how they were getting along. They were not happy people, but with few exceptions they had submitted to the commands and demands of the race that had conquered them. They were still close to their old life of freedom on the plains, deserts, and mountains, and the restrictions under which they lived had brought resentment that permanently crippled their spirit.

When we were in Oklahoma, I took time off to visit the great Apache chief Geronimo, who was a prisoner of war at Fort Sill. I had wanted to get the real story of his last struggles against the White man's soldiers. No name in the history of America's conflicts with the Indians arouses the fever to a greater pitch than that of this celebrated chief. In some books, he is described as a savage who preyed upon wagon trains and killed White travelers with abandon and fury. In those faraway days back in the last century, when the Indians were struggling for survival, the Apaches were divided into two main bands, one headed by Geronimo, and the other by Chief Cochise, who yielded to the federal government in all its demands and submitted passively to its actions. Thus, when the government sent out a detachment of soldiers to capture Geronimo, Cochise offered help. He felt that all the Apaches would be punished for the wrongs that Geronimo had done to the settlers and the wagon trains that he destroyed. His offer was rejected. The officer in charge of the federal troops was young and had just been assigned to the West. He did not know that Chief Cochise hated Geronimo. Years later I was informed by a man who was present when the officer first met Cochise that the words he used in rejecting the offer were, "Do you think I would let a murdering, thieving, savage Apache help me?"

The superintendent at Fort Sill was friendly and cooperative when I identified myself and told him I wanted to talk with Geronimo. He had an orderly bring the chief and let us sit in the patio outside his office. The chief had aged much since I last saw him. His shoulders drooped and the fire had faded from his eyes. For a while we discussed the situation of the Indians, then I asked:

"Why did Cochise and many other Apaches want to help the government capture you? Why did they hate you? What caused you to go on the warpath and kill White people who did you no harm? Why did you continue to burn their wagon trains and homes after the government promised you peace on a reservation?"

Like a man emerging from a torturing dream, his shoulders straightened and his eyes gleamed. For a moment he was too disturbed to talk. Then he said:

"Many years ago, many White men came to the Apache country. Some were good, many bad. Some of the bad ones raped my mother and my sister. My sister died and my mother cried. I was hunting, and when I returned, my mother told me what had happened."

He stopped talking and looked up at the sky and asked the blessing of the Great Spirit, then continued:

"That is why I did what I did, Red Fox. I swore to the Great Spirit that I would kill and make war on all White men who came to the land of the Apaches."

I looked at him sadly and said: "There were many who wanted to be friends of the Indians." I asked him why he did not surrender when he was surrounded in the White Mountains by troops under the direction of Generals Lawton and Shafter. For the first time he smiled, and said:

"I did not want to give them the honor of capturing me. I wanted to surrender to the one who had caused much trouble and given many headaches—General Miles. When he came, I surrendered to him in peace."

Geronimo thanked me for coming to see him, and he was pleased to learn what I had been doing. I told him I would do what I could to help get him released from prison, but he shook his head and said:

"White man never understand."

Several times I tried to get him freed, but my efforts were futile. Of all the Indians the White man feared, Geronimo was considered the worst. He had been condemned as a total, unredeemable barbarian by people who had never heard the story of the barbarity that had motivated him to revenge against everybody and everything in the White man's world.

We were playing at Cleveland, when Buffalo Bill was invited to attend a celebration in Niles, Ohio, honoring William McKinley, who had been nominated for President at the national convention of the

Republican party. They wanted him to take a group of Indians to help in the entertainment. Niles was McKinley's hometown, and he was campaigning mostly from the front porch because his wife was ill and he did not want to be away from her. If he had known that death awaited him from an assassin's bullet, he might have turned away from the honor and glory of being President of the United States.

I rounded up about forty of our show Indians and took them to Niles on two buses. We looked upon the trip as routine, as we frequently were called upon to entertain at public meetings, and Buffalo Bill thought this was good promotion for the show. We were not excited about meeting or hearing McKinley. If we had been going to see and hear Williams Jennings Bryan, who was the Democratic candidate, our interest would have been greater, for he had stirred the country with his silver-coated tongue and his pleadings for a return to religious fundamentalism. He had been called the "silver-tongued orator" through his advocacy of the free coinage of silver to replace or supplement gold. The base of the nation's currency at that time, it was being extracted from the Black Hills, where my people went to worship the Great Spirit.

That political meeting was to be stored away in my memory among cherished mementos for me to look back upon. In order to describe what happened, I must go back to the year 1847, when two events occurred that were more important than anything else since the birth of Christ; yet both went unnoticed except by a mere handful of people. Thousands of babies were born that year, near the half-century mark, but two were destined, or predestined by heredity, to capture and control light and sound. One, Thomas Alva Edison, was born at Marlin, Ohio; the other, Alexander Graham Bell, at Edinburgh, Scotland. They were honored guests at the McKinley meeting, and when they were introduced by the chairman and I saw them stand and bow like any other human being, I felt wavelets of awe sweep through my mind and spirit. I listened to the chairman speak briefly of their contributions to the progress and conveniences of mankind, but I thought how inadequate were his words. They had extended the reach of the human voice from the distance it would carry in a scream to the farthest outposts of the earth, and illuminated the night from a man reading by the light of candle or oil lamp to a white glow from electricity flaming in a glass bulb.

We were packing our equipment and getting ready to take down the tent we had put up when we saw the presidential candidate crossing the yard. He was accompanied by Buffalo Bill, Thomas Edison, and Alexander Bell, and another man who was hanging on to his arm. I yelled to the Indians to come to attention, and they gathered back of where I stood at the entrance to the tent.

"I want you to meet the coming President of your adopted country," Buffalo Bill said. "You cannot vote, but maybe he will help you get that right by the time of his second term."

The candidate cordially shook hands with me and saluted the others.

"Your show was a treat," he said. "I don't think my opponent would like it, however. He is opposed to dancing of any kind." The fourth man in the party laughed. "This is Mark Hanna, my manager," Mc-Kinley said, introducing him. "He thinks everything I say is humorous."

The manager shook hands with me, and said, "He is a good humorist, but will make a better President."

Edison and Bell then stepped forward and greeted me with handshakes, and they thanked me for our part in the entertainment. They were nearing the half-hundred-year mark, but appeared younger. Their faces fascinated me, for there was depth, serenity, and farawayness in them, and an alert interest in everything within range of their vision. They did not say anything that I recall, but they left with me an impression of greatness that made me proud of my identity within the human race.

CHAPTER XII

THE TURN OF
THE CENTURY

THE nineteenth century was nearing its end, but the United States had another war to fight before Father Time blew out the lights. The slender island of Cuba, the Gem of the Antilles, was the tinder box that would set the Western world afire, giving the United States the stature of a great power and ending the prestige of Spain on the high seas and in the councils of nations.

The Spanish-American War was in the offing in 1895 when a revolution broke out in Cuba. The United States had large investments in sugar, tobacco, and iron there, and propaganda began to build up for intervention. The entire Caribbean region was disturbed by the accusations being made against the Spanish overlords who ruled there with an iron fist. America's sympathies were with the revolutionists, and the whole nation became incensed when thousands of Cubans were rounded up by the Spanish authorities and placed in concentration camps where they died of hunger, disease, and abuses. Feelings became intensified on February 15, 1898, when the battleship *Maine* was sunk in Havana Harbor. The clamor for intervention increased and on April 11 President McKinley sent a war message to Congress, where it was immediately approved.

The war lasted only 113 days, but it presented the stage upon which one man rose to prominence. That man was Theodore Roosevelt. I had met him the fall before when he came to the opening of our show at Madison Square Garden. He was police commissioner of New York City, and Buffalo Bill had invited him as a guest. I always looked into the section reserved for distinguished visitors, and I recognized Roosevelt at once from pictures I had seen of him in newspapers. From time to time during the performance, I glanced at him because he was there watching and made it more realistic than usual. I even gave my horse an added touch of the spurs when I was riding toward the stagecoach in the holdup scene. The commissioner was standing up waving his arm. After the show ended, he came down to our tent, accompanied by Buffalo Bill and two police captains.

"Red Fox, this is Theodore Roosevelt, the police commissioner." Buffalo Bill introduced him. "He is going to arrest you for killing that stage coach driver."

"No!" the commissioner exclaimed, shaking his head, "I am going to arrest you, Bill, for killing off one of our natural resources, the buffalo." He then turned back to me and said, "I thought I knew how to ride a horse, Red Fox, but I am just a conceited amateur."

He exchanged a few remarks with others in our troop and then left with his hand on Buffalo Bill's arm. A few weeks later he came back to the show, and again visited our tent. He sat on a stool and began questioning me about horses, hunting, and the Sioux Indians. I told him about my early days in a tepee and I mentioned my uncle Crazy Horse. He smiled and said:

"Red Fox, I have always wondered how he got that name."

I explained: "I have been told that he was thrown from a colt that he tried to ride when he was three years old and landed in a clump of cactus. When he was four years old Sitting Bull and his grandmother gave him the Indian name Tashunkewitke, meaning a 'Man like a Wild Horse.'"

Roosevelt said he was planning to go elk hunting in Wyoming and invited me to go with him. I told him I never hunted. "I don't very often either," he said, and began talking about the nation's diminishing timberlands and the need for more recreational parks for the people.

He inspired me with a feeling of confidence, and I recalled what he had said when a few years later he rose to the Presidency and set aside 150 million acres of government land as a national forest reserve.

If "Teddy" Roosevelt had a character fault, it was his tendency to rattle the saber. Apparently in his nature there was a belief that people had to be restrained at times by force. He always carried a big stick, and even used it as police commissioner against criminals, making the metropolis a safer place for its inhabitants.

When the war broke out, he quickly recruited a regiment of horsemen from Western cowboys and New York polo players and led them into the field of battle. He was a swashbuckling figure with his broad-brimmed hat, tortoise-shell glasses, and mustached face, his smile showing prominent teeth. The newspapers found him to be colorful copy, and after his intrepid Rough Riders stormed a Spanish bastion on San Juan Hill, he became a national hero.

When the war started, patriotism was at fever pitch in America and thousands of men flocked into recruiting offices the next morning. The spirit influenced the Indians in the show, and many left to enter the service. Buffalo Bill did not raise any objections when I told him I was enlisting, but wished me good luck and invited me to rejoin the show when I returned. He said he intended to close the show and would join the army as a scout if they would take him.

Because of my experience at sea, I was advised by the recruiting office to join the Navy, which I did; and after a few weeks of training, I was assigned to a battleship. We sailed from Boston and cruised along the coast of Cuba, but by that time the war was over, and we were sent to the Orient with the Pacific fleet, where we visited China, Japan, and the Philippines. I was discharged at Mare Island on May 10, 1902.

Theodore Roosevelt was President, and I thought about going to Washington to see him. I knew he would give me a job, but I was not eager to go back to work for the government after living a regulated and disciplined life for so many moons. I could rejoin the show, but decided to stay in the West for at least a year. I wanted to be near the ocean which I had come to admire. It was as personal as a virgin in love and as unpredictable as a storm playing roulette with the waves. I had not saved any money in the service, so after idling and talking to every Indian I met, I applied for a job at a shipping office and was accepted for a place as second mate on a packet steamer on a run between Alaska and Pacific Coast ports. We had made several round trips, and were unloading a cargo at the docks in San Francisco early one afternoon when my attention was attracted by a man about my own age who was sitting on an empty keg, watching the operation and taking notes. I thought he might be a detective checking our cargo for contraband; so for a while I watched him, and then went down the gangplank and sauntered leisurely toward him. He was dressed in a leather jacket and overalls. His shoulders were broad and his head crowned with an abundance of dark hair that curled around the edges of the old sea cap he was wearing. There was curiosity in his eyes as he glanced up at me and said, "Hello!"

"*Buenos días,*" I greeted him.

"Spanish?" he questioned; then he said, "No, Indian, aren't you?"

"Yes, Sioux," I said. "Chief Red Fox."

He stood up and shook hands with me. "A chief, uh?" and he smiled. "I have an Indian in the story I am writing."

"You are a writer, then, not a policeman?" I asked.

Again he laughed. "That's one for the book. I'll have to tell my friends about that." He paused, staring at me. "Pardon me, Chief. I am glad to meet you. My name is London—Jack London. People, especially readers and some friends, have called me everything from a tramp to an alcoholic, but never a policeman."

"I have read a few of your stories," I told him. "I like the way you tell about policemen and sailors. You seem to know a lot about them."

"I should! I have sailed and hoboed, and been in jail," he said.

"I guess you have to do things and live with people to write about them, don't you?" I asked.

"Yes, but you don't have to be like people, thank God! I am writing a book about the life of people at sea. That's why I am here today. I want to pick out a few characters—now you walk into my story like something out of the past—a real Indian chief."

I told him I was the nephew of Chief Crazy Horse.

"He licked the hell out of Custer, didn't he? I have always admired him."

He put the notebook and pencil into his pockets and invited me to have coffee or a mug of beer with him at a small dockside restaurant. I went willingly, for I needed a break in a day during which I had no duties. Once in the restaurant with schooners of foaming beer on the table, he began asking me about my life aboard ship, and the experiences I had in the ports we visited. He questioned me about how people behaved during a storm and what the sailors discussed in their quarters. He seemingly was probing into what our thoughts and emotions were under trial and stress, as well as during our leisure hours. Occasionally he would break into his questions to tell an episode from his own life—like the time when, as a boy, he robbed oyster nets in San Francisco Bay until the police suspected him and he had to go into hiding. He told me that he was born in 1876—the year of the Custer battle. It was an auspicious year for people who liked his writings, and I told him so.

"It was not auspicious for the Sioux," he said, and began asking me questions about my childhood and youth.

After he had explored that subject, he began to tell me about his own struggles with poverty and deprivations as a boy. And out of this came the conclusion that he was driven to write in order to win fame and meet prominent people.

We had three or four beers and our conversation gradually vanished into a vague unremembered haze, and I was back aboard ship with a splitting headache.

Some years later when I heard of his death, I recalled that sunny afternoon in San Francisco, and I wondered if he had taken his own life because of the shattering of illusions that had intrigued and sustained him as he was reaching up toward the stars.

CHAPTER XIII

TO KILL
A KING

I REJOINED the show in the spring of 1903 at Madison Square Garden. Buffalo Bill greeted me with the affection of a father for a prodigal son. Time, the versatile artist of destiny, had been sketching on his face while I was away. He looked older and had gained weight in areas where it settles comfortably as a companion of age; but it had not dimmed the eagerness with which he reached out to captivate the world.

"We've made some changes in the show since you left, Red Fox," he said, after we talked briefly about our intimate selves. "We've hired a new stage manager. Get acquainted with him. Tell him to put you back in the dances and the holdup. Maybe he can work out a new routine for you—something about your hitch in Davy Jones's locker."

The manager was an angular, red-headed youth,

as nervous as a mentally disturbed cat. He was working on a booklet when I entered his office and introduced myself. He welcomed me absently, and I could see that his thoughts were still concentrated on the booklet, which he confirmed by saying:

"Why don't you loaf around for a few days, Chief, until we get the show started? We are at the peak of annoyances right now. Sit in at the opening tomorrow night as a critic."

I told him I would enjoy being a spectator.

"Come in and see me the morning after," he said, and turned back to his work.

Most of the Indians who were in the show when I enlisted were gone. Buffalo Bill had recruited new ones from several different tribes and reservations. I talked to some of them, but they looked upon me as just another Indian, and I felt deflated. Perhaps I needed applause for winning the Spanish-American War. Mainly though, I was lonesome. During that afternoon, I went out and tanked up on a few beers.

The next day I felt better, after having adjusted my thinking, and I was in the reserved section at 7:30 P.M. when I heard the familiar calling of the bugle and the low beat of tom-toms that signaled the opening. My pulse rate increased by a few beats as the lights were dimmed and a group of Indians came into the arena and started putting up a tepee. I was only mildly interested, however, until the spotlight focused on the stage where a cowboy was twirling a lariat. I soon realized that he was an artist with the rope. He was chewing gum and chattering like a squirrel. I did not hear his first words, but then his voice came clearly: "All I know is what I read in the papers." His words seemed synchronized with the dexterous movements of the lariat. I bent forward, looking and listening. He began commenting and joking about prominent people and current events with wit that brought smiles and occasional ripples of laughter from the audience. There was satire too, in what he said, devastating satire that made his personality luminous.

When he finished his act, there was a burst of applause. I glanced at the program to see who he was: "Will Rogers, Lariat-Lingo Artist." I had never heard of Will Rogers, but I knew that he had something that most entertainers lacked—profound concentration in what he was doing, and unusual skill in doing it. He inspired me to perfect my skill with a rope. I knew some tricks that he had not used in his act, and I could do them on horseback where I would not have to talk. I was aware of my limitations. I could tell a joke from memory, but there was serene wisdom under the satire and humor I had heard that night from a man who could have entertained even if he had left his lariat on the range.

A few days later we met in a coffee shop where I had gone after the show. He entered with Buffalo Bill, and they sat at my table.

"This is Chief Red Fox. He was with us until the war broke out," said Buffalo Bill as he introduced us. "He's been in the Navy. You two should be congenial if a Sioux and Cherokee ever can be."

"I knew by your regalia that you were a Sioux," Rogers said. "You have an advantage over me—I'm only part Redskin."

"How big a part?" I asked.

"An eighth, or thereabouts, but one drop would set me to braggin'. "

"It hasn't always been that way, has it?" I commented. "But you were raised with the Whites. I came out of a tepee."

"That must have been about the time your people clobbered Custer, Red Fox. Do you remember that?"

For at least a half-hour we sat there talking about Indian history and related subjects, and I learned that both his parents had Indian blood, and that he was born on a ranch near Claremont, Oklahoma, and was educated at a military academy. After graduation, he went to the Texas panhandle, where he learned to use a lariat. Four years later, he shipped to Argentina on a cattle boat and then joined a circus, where he was billed as "The Oklahoma Kid."

Buffalo Bill, who was always on the lookout for new talent, saw his act and offered him more money, which proved to be smart business, for Rogers soon began getting mention in theatre columns, and people went to the show just to see and hear him.

By the time the session broke up that night, we had established a communion that lasted as long as

Will Rogers lived. He was with us only a few months when Flo Ziegfeld came to our show one night while we were playing in Philadelphia. Ziegfeld had produced the lavish spectacle at the World's Fair in Chicago and was bringing sensational innovations to the vaudeville stage. He was planning his masterpiece, the "Ziegfeld Follies," and wanted the best talent he could find. He literally took Rogers back to New York with him. In the metropolis, with the world waiting as a theatre and the great producer in the wings, Rogers rose rapidly to stardom. He played in Eugene O'Neill's drama, *Ah, Wilderness,* and became a familiar figure on the silver screen.

Occasionally I saw him, and he always welcomed me graciously and warmly. He was vitally interested in the affairs and problems of the Indians. I felt a deep sorrow when he was killed in an airplane crash at Point Barrow, Alaska, in 1935, while on the way to the Orient with Wiley Post. He had achieved lasting greatness during his lifetime, not as a lariat twirler or even as a humorist, for this was merely the frosting on his philosophy. It was the depth of his wisdom that left an impression on the blueprint of time; and this is expressed in a statue of him in the Capitol at Washington where other celebrated personalities in the history of America are displayed in marble and bronze.

We traveled across the United States and Canada that summer and fall of 1904 and holed up in winter quarters in late October. Buffalo Bill was planning to take the show to Europe the next spring, and asked me to help in the preparations.

We had everything in readiness when on a morning in March, 1905, we sailed past the Statue of Liberty on the steamship *Nebraska,* headed for Liverpool.

It is doubtful if a ship has ever sailed over the ocean with a stranger cargo and passenger list since Noah set adrift in the Ark. Our horses were stabled in the ship's hold, along with some mules, two donkeys, and a half-dozen long-horned steers. The Indians occupied quarters in the stern, with the rest of the company in the fo'c'sle, except the captain and his officers, who had cabins on the upper deck. Our tents and props were stored compactly wherever space could be found.

I had taken some books and magazines aboard, and spent much of my time reading and writing about experiences I remembered from the time I was a child. Even then I thought of writing a book some day, but I did not imagine that nearly three-quarters of a century would pass before I had it ready for publication. The sea appeared in vagrant moods during the thirteen days it took us to make the trip. At times it stretched before us in an unbroken panorama of quietness, and again in a veil of mists and clouds; or the wind hurried across it, bringing rollers that rocked the ship and splashed over its main deck. The sun, moon, and stars gave me companionship. Once in a while, a giant fish or whale or shark would break through the surface as if coming up to investigate our ship, and perhaps to wonder about such a strange creature invading its watery domain.

The advance men had prepared for our arrival, and soon we were established in a comfortable camp on the Thames River, not far from Westminster Abbey, where we were scheduled to open three days later.

In those days at the beginning of the twentieth century, London had not changed much from what it was when Charles Dickens created Tiny Tim, old Scrooge, and Little Nell. I was bewitched by that prolific English novelist whose imaginary characters seemed more real to me than the real characters who swarmed around our encampment. Mainly, however, he impressed me with his efforts to lessen the cruelty and inhumanity with which children were treated. I had been brought up in an environment that was a paradise compared with this author's early life labeling bottles in a warehouse, or his characterization of the brutalities of the monstrous schoolmaster Squeers in *Nicholas Nickleby*. I visited London through the scenes and the people in his books. I took long walks through the streets as we waited for the opening, and the past which he had pictured dominated the present; but I knew that many reforms had come about through his vivid writings.

When friends ask me about some of the greatest thrills of my life, I tell them that one of them took place in London. It began an hour before the opening show. I was sitting on a stool at the entrance to a tepee when I saw Buffalo Bill walking toward me with another man who was dressed in boots, cowboy hat, and buckskin suit, with two guns hanging around his waist.

I wondered who the man was, and as they came closer I could see his face clearly. I thought I recognized him, but I could not believe what I saw. I struggled from my comfortable stool and was standing when Buffalo Bill brought me to quick military attention.

"Chief Red Fox," he said, "this is His Majesty, Edward the Seventh, King of England."

I was about to stretch out my hand to shake hands, but the king gave me a military salute, which I returned. Then he turned to Buffalo Bill. "Not only the King of England, Bill," he said, smiling broadly, "but of Great Britain, Ireland, and dominions beyond the seas, including India and Canada, by the grace of God."

"My pardon, Your Majesty," Buffalo Bill replied lightly.

The king laughed, and put his hand on Buffalo Bill's arm.

"Chief," he addressed me, "I have been looking forward to this day with much pleasure. I want you Redskins to put on a bloody good fight tonight when you hold up the stagecoach. Bill and I will be in the coach."

The holdup was at the closing of each show, a dramatic, breath-taking scene planned to give spectators something to remember and talk about after they left the show.

I was in this act along with Chiefs Pine Bird and Standing Bear, and when I told them what the King had said, they took the news as stoically as they did everything, but Standing Bear grunted, "Heap big chief. We fix him plenty good."

"I will take care of the King. You get Buffalo Bill, Standing Bear, and you the driver, Pine Bird," I told them.

We were waiting when the signal came for the stagecoach attack. The lights were dimmed as we entered the arena spurring our horses and whooping. We circled the coach with flaming arrows in our hands, which we fired into cans of powder that exploded and lighted the coach as if it were on fire. Several other Indians stopped the coach horses, yanked the passengers out, and killed them with realistic effects.

Standing Bear slugged the driver with a rubber tomahawk. Pine Bird grabbed Buffalo Bill and disposed of him with equal effect as the spectators sat spellbound. I left His Majesty for the final touch of drama. Bill had told me that the people did not know their King would be in the coach, but when I jerked him out and they saw who he was, they screamed bloody murder. As I raised the tomahawk to complete the illusion of a savage on the warpath, I paused an instant to accentuate the drama, then brought the death-dealing instrument against the monarch's balding head. The smack was like a firecracker exploding, and a roar of mingled distress and amusement billowed through the arena.

Quickly the scene dissolved. The lights came on, and our first performance in Europe was up to the expectations of our promoters, who had persuaded the King to take part in it. The news of the act spread over Europe on the "talking wires" and set the stage for our appearance in all the big cities of the Continent. For me personally, it was a moment of vicarious exultation, and I thought that perhaps a strain of suppressed malignancy lingered in my veins from ancestors who had been accused many times of scalping innocent White men, but never of blackjacking one with a rubber tomahawk.

After the show the King came to our big tepee and talked freely with the Indians. He told us about playing poker with some of our cowboys and Buffalo Bill the night before. He called it the "game of the cowboys," and said it was great when he was winning. He dispelled the last illusion we had about the divine or superhuman attributes with which people vest royalty. He was entirely human, and we would have immediately accepted him as a big chief.

In 1901 he had ascended to the throne after the death of his famous mother, Queen Victoria. Before that time, he became widely known as one of England's leading sportsmen. He had a stable of the fastest horses in Europe. He visited Canada when he was twenty years old and learned about the struggles and plight of the Indians.

It was not until I learned these facts about him that I was able to understand how he could step down from the throne so easily to fraternize with Indians in their tepee and enjoy a part in the scene they were enacting.

Buffalo Bill had planned to spend only one season in Europe, but it was four years before we returned to America. Everywhere we went, people flocked to our show by the thousands, especially to see the Indians and cowboys. We added new stunts to our repertoire from time to time. I had been practicing with the lariat and learned to rope a steer while hanging to a running horse with my heel over the saddle horn, and my body extending over the side of the animal. I could also fire an arrow from that precarious position and put it in a bull's-eye. The act brought applause, but the stage holdup was always the highlight of the show.

I obtained a liberal education about the people, geography, and historical places of Europe during those years. Of all the countries where we played, Ireland charmed me the most. We played in Dublin, Cork, and Galway, and walked along the banks of the picturesque river Shannon, which was popularized and romanticized later in the song "Where the River Shannon Flows." I was enamored of the little town of Tipperary, which became popular among Allied soldiers in World War I in "It's a Long Way to Tipperary." I saw the ruins of Muckross Abbey in Killarney, and the marble quarries and coal mines near Kilkenny, a city of about 10,000, where the expression to "quarrel like Kilkenny cats" originated because of its citizens' bitter feud with the people of a neighboring city.

The Irish people were living as they had for hundreds of years. Most of them were on small plots of land where they grew potatoes and a few lesser crops. Their small white cottages dotted the land. I could see why the name Emerald Isle was applied to their land, and why it cast a spell over its inhabitants and called them back with homesickness after they had moved away. This emotion has become a familiar theme in Irish poetry and songs and is reflected in America and other lands on St. Patrick's Day, when people wear the shamrock or a green garment in response to the romanticism which it inspires in their minds and hearts.

In Carlisle, I had read Longfellow's poems "Hiawatha" and "The Courtship of Miles Standish," and on the way to Europe I decided to visit the grave of Pocahontas. The opportunity came on a weekend when we were camped near Gloucester, and the show would not open for several days. I made my way to Crews, and just before noon on a Sunday afternoon, I stood looking down on a tiny plot of land—the final resting place of that famous Indian girl.

An old caretaker who greeted me said that many

visitors went to see where Pocahontas was buried. "She was the first American to become a Lady of England," he said.

Books are not entirely factual in telling the story of the time when Pocahontas was held hostage on an English ship in an effort to bring about peace terms with the Indians who were attacking the colony fellow Englishmen had established at Jamestown.

The dramatic series of events that centered around her started when a English sailing ship came across Chesapeake Bay and dropped anchor at the mouth of a river, named James after their reigning King. They were welcomed by the Indians and their chief, Powhatan, and decided to found a colony near the estuary of the river.

The Indians brought food to the settlers and taught them about the country, but antagonisms soon developed between the two races who were so far apart in their ways of living. Powhatan was first to realize that they were threatened by the invaders who were trespassing on their land and destroying its wild game and other resources, so he decided to drive them out. In that effort, he was helped by the Chickahominy Indians led by Chief Opechancanough.

Pocahontas was the favorite daughter of Chief Powhatan. She was twelve or thirteen years old when the English arrived. She visited them on their ship and met John Smith, their leader. She fell in love with him and he became enamored of her. Following a mutiny aboard the ship, Smith was deposed, and in the months that followed he explored the countryside and obtained food and other supplies from the Indians. On one of those expeditions he was captured by the Chickahominy Indians and condemned to death. When Pocahontas heard of this, she pleaded with her father to save Smith's life. He could not deny her wishes and intervened, but Chief Opechancanough refused to listen. When the time for the execution came and the ax was about to fall, Pocahontas flung her body upon Smith, and his life was saved. Her act inspired both the Indians and the colonists, and peace was restored; but when Smith returned to England a few months later, hostilities broke out again. The commander in charge at Jamestown realized that the safety of the colonists depended upon Pocahontas, who had become a heroine, not only among the Indians, but with the colonists. He managed to lure her aboard the ship and held her hostage for more than a year while peace terms were being negotiated. On the ship Pocahontas attracted the attention of John Rolfe, who fell in love with her. When she questioned him about Smith, he is reported to have told her that Smith was dead. Not long after that she and Rolfe were married, and she declared that the settlers and the Indians should live as brothers and friends. The following year the couple sailed for England, and on their arrival she was greeted as a princess and introduced at the Court of King James, and made a Lady of England. There she came face-to-face with John Smith, the man she really loved. When she asked her husband why he had told her Smith was dead, he replied, "Because I loved you as you loved him."

Disillusioned, Pocahontas wanted to return to her native home, but she was pregnant and had to wait until the child was born. The child was a boy who was named after his father. When the child was old enough to travel, Pocahontas pleaded with her husband to allow her to return to Virginia.

"You can go back to the savages," he told her, "but you will never take my son."

She appealed to the Queen, who said she would talk to the King and get permission for her to return to her native land, if possible. King James agreed and arranged for her passage. Again she asked Rolfe to allow her to take the child with her, and again he refused. Soon after this the King and Queen sent Pocahontas to Gravesend, where she would go aboard ship for the voyage back home. While waiting for the ship to sail, she was stricken with smallpox and died on March 21, 1617. She was buried in the Church of England's graveyard at Crews.

Many years later when I was in Richmond, Virginia, to address a Boy Scout meeting, I was surprised by the conversation of several fashionably dressed women in the lobby of the hotel where I was stopping. One of them strolled over to me and, pointing to a woman in the group, asked, "Do you know who she is, Chief?"

I replied, "No, who is she?"

"She is the first Virginian and American to become a Lady of England," she said with great pride.

"Is she Pocahontas?" I asked.

The woman looked at me strangely and said, "That is Lady Astor."

"Oh," I said, "you don't know your state or American history."

With that she turned away angrily and joined the others. I heard her repeat what I had said, and then Lady Astor spoke: "Chief Red Fox is right. Pocahontas was the first American to be named a Lady of England. She was called Rebecca."

CHAPTER XIV

TEPEES IN THE
NICKELODEON

BEFORE we took our show to Germany, I visited a library to learn something about the country and its royal family. The Indians were always featured in advance publicity, and our big tepee was a sort of living museum that attracted high officials wherever we went. On the afternoon before the opening in Berlin, Buffalo Bill told me to prepare to receive the Kaiser and the Prince. I told the Indians to put on their war bonnets and other regalia and be seated in a circle, as if in council, when the visitors arrived. I was waiting at the door of the tepee when I saw the Kaiser and his young son crossing the lot with Buffalo Bill and four uniformed bodyguards. The Kaiser was around thirty years old, and was wearing a cape over his uniform that concealed his crippled arm. His son was about nine or ten years old.

Buffalo Bill introduced them as "the Emperor of Germany and the Crown Prince," and he introduced me as "Chief Red Fox of the Sioux Nation." They saluted me formally, and in broken German I welcomed them with "Indians welcome heap big chiefs for council." I held open the door of the tepee, and bowed ceremoniously for them to enter. Buffalo Bill winked slyly at me as he followed them through the doorway.

The Kaiser paused for a moment looking down at the Indians who were passing a peace pipe around the circle. Then he stepped forward with his son and sat down where a place had been left for them. The Indians were hunched over with their legs crossed, and the Kaiser and his son quickly imitated them.

In silence they sat as the pipe was passed from mouth to mouth, and each took a puff when it came to them. Then Standing Bear arose and bowed before the Kaiser. He had a new pipe of peace in his hand, which was decorated with a blue ribbon. "Indians give peace offering to visiting big chief," he said and held out the pipe. "Indians never go on warpath against braves of German tribe."

The Kaiser broke into a hearty laugh, then extended his hand and accepted the pipe. "German soldiers never fight Indians—only French and English," he said. "Tell this to your people when you return to your hunting grounds."

The Kaiser handed the pipe to his son as they turned to leave, and seeing me standing at attention

[1 5 1]

near the door, he reached out his free hand and shook mine. "Many thanks, Chief," he said. "That was a more friendly reception than I receive in some courts."

When we finished our tour of Germany and crossed the border into Italy, misfortune awaited us. We were preparing for the opening in Rome when one of our horses was stricken with distemper. Buffalo Bill called a veterinarian to treat the horse, and he promptly quarantined our show, and there we remained completely immobilized for nine weeks. We never performed there. In October, when we were released, it was time to head for Marseilles, where we were to spend a few months in winter quarters and plan for our next season's tour. We were not allowed, however, to cross the border until Buffalo Bill paid the customs officials $8,000 in American money. He did not have that much with him, and had to telegraph to America for it.

We camped outside the border for a week until a bank in Paris sent us the money on instructions from America. Immediately after we entered France, we were surrounded by police who seized all our horses, which were among the best-trained animals in the world. Many of them were owned by the cowboys and Indian performers. I owned three—two for trick roping and one for my pleasure.

Buffalo Bill tried to get them released, but no one in power would budge an inch. We could never figure out if the animals were seized because of the quarantine in Italy or if that was an excuse for confiscating them. I do remember that, after days of futile efforts, Buffalo Bill refused to eat meat in any restaurant, saying he did not care for horse steak.

That experience, and the long enforced idleness in Italy, had sapped most of Buffalo Bill's available funds, and he decided to close the show and return to America. It is doubtful if a traveling troupe ever broke up with greater distress. None of us had much pocket money, our horses were gone, and no one knew what would happen when we returned to the States.

We loaded the tents, seats, saddles, covered wagons, and other properties on a J. P. Morgan steamship that was sailing for Philadelphia, and embarked on a small passenger ship bound for Liverpool. We were relieved to get aboard and watch the land of France fade into a blur along the horizon.

Buffalo Bill raised funds in Liverpool to pay our way to Philadelphia on the steamship *Marion*. We arrived on March 6 and went to our old winter quarters at the fair grounds in Trenton, New Jersey. There we were greeted by Pawnee Bill, who had been elected mayor under his English name, Gordon Lillie. He said that during our absence seven Wild West shows had sprung up. He owned one of them and invited Buffalo Bill to join with him and call their show "Buffalo Bill of the Wild West and Pawnee Bill of the Far East." Pawnee Bill had the railroad cars, horses, and other equipment that could

[1 5 3]

be combined with ours to make the best show in the field. He also had funds to launch the project; so Buffalo Bill signed a contract with him. The show prospered until Pawnee Bill retired four years later. Buffalo Bill then signed a contract with the Sells Floto Circus for the seasons of 1914 and 1915. Most of the equipment he owned had been sold at auction to pay off his debts. He was seventy-eight years old, and the glamor that had once sheltered and enriched his life on the high pinnacle of showmanship was all but gone, but he clung to the prestige that remained, and in 1916 he was connected briefly with the 101 Ranch Wild West Show. He made his last public appearance on October 6, that year, and then went to live with his sister in Denver, Colorado. He died on January 10, the next year, and was buried with respect and honors on Lookout Mountain. In my imagination, I can see his noble spirit winging over the lofty peak, and I bow my head in memory of one who always impressed me with kindness and compassion, and enriched me with the deeply entrenched integrity of his character.

Upon our return from Europe, I had received an invitation to join the Miller Brothers' 101 Ranch. They offered me more money than Pawnee Bill would pay; so I went with them and remained until we went into winter quarters at Venice, California, in the fall of 1910. While we were there, Thomas H. Ince, a moving picture director, came to our quarters and asked me to help him get together a group of

Indians and Mexicans to play in a series of Western movies he was planning to produce. Many of those in the ranch show welcomed the opportunity to go into an entertainment field that was supplanting the road show and even encroaching on the domain of the regular theatre. Nickelodeons were springing up all over the country, and the prices, as well as the sensational pictures, were attracting countless people who had never seen a Wild West show or the inside of a theatre.

I signed a contract with Ince, and appeared in ten pictures, mostly in holdup and war scenes where I was just part of the action. The stars were Grace Cunard, Frances Ford, J. Barney Sherley, and "Shorty" Hamilton. The first picture was *War on the Plains* and it showed much more finesse than the reality it was supposed to portray. The script writers had enhanced the actual happenings with romance and drama, and our arrows always hit the mark.

Then I accepted an offer to join the Selig Studio in Chicago. Their stars were Myrtle Stedman, Kathryn Williams, William Duncan, and William Stowell. I played a secondary role in *When the Heart Calls* and did nine other pictures with Bronco Billy—Gilbert Anderson—where I was indentifiable on the screen.

My next experience in motion pictures was with Warner Brothers, where I appeared in *Daughters of the Tribe, Toll of the Warpath, Red Fox and Wild Flower, Perils of the Plains,* and *Medicine Boy.*

[1 5 5]

There too, if a nickelodeon viewer knew me beforehand, he could have picked me out among the other actors, but not in a star role.

I must have been ascending in importance, for I was invited to work with William S. Hart, who was on the payroll of Triangle Production Company. I came into view clearly as a supporting actor in *The Covered Wagon* with J. Warren Kerigan, Alan Hale, and Ernest Torrance in three pictures; and with Richard Dix and Malcolm McGregor in *The Vanishing American.* The company sent me out on the road, and later put me in *Desert Gold* with William Powell and *The Wild Horse Massacre* with Jack Holt. I also had minor parts in *The Flaming Arrow* and *The Law of Crippled Creek.*

My star in the movies never rose far above the horizon, but I did get somewhere near the top in *The Round Up,* where my name appeared on the billboards along with Slim Hoover, Florence Rockwell, and Maclyn Arbuckle. Those pictures were mostly one- and two-reelers in which I engaged in savage attacks on wagon trains, ambushed White troops, set fire to the homes of White settlers, and lassoed a terrified buffalo calf while galloping on a horse. I was pictured in war dances that a script writer must have dreamed up while in a nightmare. I also scalped a missionary with a rubber tomahawk that squirted a red fluid resembling blood when his skull was hit.

Those scenes reflected the public's opinion of the Indian and stirred the emotions of audiences. Usually something was injected into the scenario showing an Indian getting barbecued for his crimes, and relieving the morbid tensions that were built up in those early nickeldeon melodramas.

There were times when I wanted to go down to a clean stream and wash away my duplicity, but I had been under the klieg lights a long time, and realized that I could do little to change opinions that were rigidly fixed from the preceding centuries.

Between the picture making in 1929 and 1930 I lectured on the "Lost Chautauqua" circuit out of Bloomington, Illinois. The circuit was owned by the evangelist Billy Sunday and Ruth Bryan, daughter of William Jennings Bryan. Miss Bryan had been elected to the United States House of Representatives from Florida. She was a fluent speaker, and I have always felt that my appearance on the same platform with her, which I did for several weeks, left much to be desired. It was a devastating experience. My Indian costume helped, and I managed to hold the attention of audiences by talking about growing up in a tepee and conversing with the crowned heads of Europe.

Billy Sunday had reached the cloudless atmosphere of evangelism, and crowds swarmed to hear him. The Chautauqua was a sideline for him, for he lectured in the largest tabernacles. He arranged to have sawdust spread on the floor, if possible, wherever he preached; so when sinners went up to the altar they were said to be "hitting the sawdust trail." I saw him a few times, but he was always on the run, although he did stop long enough once to warn me about the weakness of all flesh, including mine, after he saw me smoking a cigar.

I cannot report that I liked lecturing, for my tongue has never been clever in speech or subtle in repartee; nor was I endowed by creation with the spiritualistic fervor that underlies evangelism. Billy Sunday and Ruth Bryan possessed these attributes in rich measure, and I envied them the gifts of eloquence with which they brought sinners to their knees. The lecturing did, however, help prepare me for the work I began the following year as an ambassador of good will for a large corporation.

I was close to sixty years old when I entered that new field, and I am still at it almost forty years later. I have been doing what I can, not only to promote the corporation, but to help the younger generation understand the verities that must be observed to achieve self-respect and happiness. I have lectured in many schools and at conferences of Boy and Girl Scouts, and I have been interviewed on television, radio, and by newspapers all over the United States and Canada—and even in Europe and the Hawaiian Islands.

CHAPTER XV

EQUATING
THE SAVAGE

ALMOST every day of my life since I finished
school someone has asked me about the Indians. If I
counted only one question a day, the total would be
nearly 30,000, but this should be multiplied by at
least 5, bringing the number to 150,000. In my appearances at school, Scout meetings, social events, before legislative meetings, and while riding on trains
and airplanes, I have always been in Indian dress and
people have gravitated to me and asked questions as
they would turn to an encyclopedia for information
about something they wanted to know.

Time after time people have asked me what the
Indians had of value to give other people of the
world. That question was easy to answer, for the natives of this continent who lived in peace and security
before Columbus discovered it on his way to India had
a menu of many foods that were unknown anywhere

else in the world. Those included corn, string beans, peanuts, cocoa, tapioca, turnips, squash, yams, potatoes, pumpkins, melons, turkeys, and oysters. These foods were served around their campfires. They had vanilla and sarsaparilla, made from leaves and roots of plants found originally in America.

In medicine, they were ingenious in using the trees, plants, and grasses of their environment to provide for the treatment of injuries and diseases. Among those were cocaine, an extract of cocoa leaves; and quinine, from the bark of the cinchona tree.

They made garments from the wool and fur of many animals, and even from the feathers of the birds and the skins of fish. The hardy vicuña that lives only in the high Andes Mountains was shorn for its wool, which was spun into cloth by their ancient weavers; and the alpaca, another ruminant found only in South America, provided a fine wool that the natives made into clothing. The fur of the beaver, bear, fox, elk and caribou, and even the buffalo, was a dependable source of supplies for Indians of the plains, providing them with food for their tables, fur for their clothing, hides for their tepees, and chips for heating their homes.

One of the native products that has become known throughout the entire world is tobacco, which manufacturers and dealers have made billions of dollars on. The Indians used this weed in their religious ceremonies, as it was almost a sacred plant. The peace pipe in which they smoked the tobacco signified good will, and its smoke rising toward the heavens was an appeal for a blessing from the Great Spirit. There was no evidence that the native Americans ever indulged in its use for pleasure.

When the Pilgrims landed on these shores in 1620, the Indians taught them how to make snow shoes from birch bark, and canoes from the strong bark of beech trees that grew in abundance on the Eastern coast. The Tuscaroras taught the immigrants from Europe how to make rope and mats from the hemp which they cultivated and harvested.

Most of all, the Indians gave the first settlers a sanctuary from the political and religious tyranny they had suffered in the Old World. The conflicts that followed have been told and retold many times with variations, so I will not further recount them here. I can sum it up by repeating the words of Chief Charging Hawk, spoken when I was riding beside him during a parade at Plymouth, Massachusetts.

"Here is where the Pilgrims landed." Then he smiled, but there was a trace of regretful fatality in his face as he continued: "When they came, they fell upon their knees; then they fell upon the aborigines with shotguns on their shoulders, flasks of whiskey on their hips, and Bibles under their arms."

Why did the Indians and the White men have wars?

That was one of the questions most often asked, especially after I had presented a talk to students or a troop of Boy or Girl Scouts.

The wars never would have occurred if the White man had not invaded the homelands of the Indians, endangered their livelihood, corrupted them with whiskey, and treated them as pagans and savages. That sounds like a brutal evaluation of what happened, but it is coming through the mists of time as the final conclusion of history. It is the deep, underlying cause of every battle fought by the Indians against the settlers and the government troops that supported them at every crossroad where the Indians were being forced to relinquish their lands. They attacked and burned settlements, but the White man would have done the same if squatters had invaded his homeland and threatened his security. Blaming the Indians for those wars is like blaming the simple soil tillers of Vietnam for the flames and bullets that are devastating their homeland.

"Weren't the Indians on reservations protected by the government?"

Young students are taught to be patriotic and to believe in the integrity of their country, and I have been discreet in answering that question. Sometimes I have quoted the words of Stephen Decatur: "Our country . . . may she always be in the right; but our country, right or wrong."

Actually the conduct of agents in the early days and their support of traders is a story of looting, thievery, and conspiracy almost without parellel. For many years the Department of Indian Affairs was a political bureau through which appointments were made to satisfy henchmen of the party in power. In most cases, the appointees, including the reservation agents, were illiterate and unscrupulous and had no comprehension of the Indian as anything more than a savage who could be plundered without fear. Those henchmen had votes and were more important than the welfare of a group of painted savages who could not vote and whose rights could be violated with impunity.

There were countless occasions when Indian agents cooperated with trading companies who wanted to stop immigrants from settling in the West so that they could keep control of the lands where they were entrenched. As long as they could do that, and there were few laws, they could trade, jump claims, sell liquor to the Indians, and in fact do just about as they pleased. Often the field men of those trading companies committed felonies against the settlers, for example, stealing horses or setting fire to their homes, then blaming the Indians.

Many of the reservation agents enriched themselves by selling food, clothing and blankets, and other commodities that the government had issued for distribution among the Indians. When the Indians protested the wrongs, the agents would cry to the government that the Indians were on the warpath. The government would send troops to quell them, and that would be the last heard about the atrocities and robberies. If the Indians raised crops or stock, the agents, whose control was arbitrary, marketed the surpluses at a profit for themselves.

I was given the opportunity to discuss those conditions on August 24, 1924, when I was invited to address a joint session of the United States Congress. I was introduced by Vice-President Charles Curtis, whose mother was of Cherokee descent. I spoke about the country's treatment of the Indians and appealed to Congress to grant them citizenship rights and protect them by ending the practice of parceling out the reservations, giving land-grabbers a chance to stupefy them with whiskey and then get hold of their property. I also pointed out the need for reforms in the Bureau of Indian Affairs, and for appointing better qualified men to take charge of the reservations and agencies.

Under the Coolidge-Curtis administration conditions improved, and the Indians were granted citizenship, but it was not until Franklin D. Roosevelt was elected President that the old order was thrown out and better life presumed for the Indians.

Roosevelt was a good friend of the Indians. He had tried to relieve them of the political tyrannies to which they were subjected before he went to Washington. Soon after he took office, he appointed John Collier as Commissioner of Indian Affairs and asked him to reform the service and relieve it of the inefficiency and corruption that had made it a disgrace to the nation and a disaster for the Indians. Collier was a noted authority on the history of the Indians and the nation's treatment of them after they were conquered.

He had organized the American Indian Defense Association in New York City and was its executive secretary. Nationally known authors, businessmen, and professors served on the board of that organization, including Mary Austin, author of *The Land of Little Rain* and many articles about native Americans; Dr. Haven Emerson, professor of surgery at Columbia University; and L. R. E. Paulin, chief editorial writer for the New York *World*. Collier had the support of many congressmen through which he was able to rid the service of the riff-raff that had dominated it since its beginning. He improved educational facilities and health services on the reservations and instituted regulations and laws to protect the Indian in his property and to provide opportunities for him to become more active in the affairs of the nation.

"How do the Indians receive their names?"

That is another question that I have often been asked by students. They want to know especially how I came to be named Red Fox.

Some writers, speculating on this, have said that the Indian child is named after some animal or bird that he dreamed of killing. Reason quickly dispels that fiction, for Indian children are named for things they would not have been likely to dream about. I am not writing about Indians who live on reservations, or in close relationship with White people, where they usually have Christian names; but about those who were living when I was born a century ago, and long before that. There are countless thousands of half-blooded Indians today who could not answer that question, nor could they explain why the Indians painted their faces, why they wore feathers, why they buried their dead the way they did, or what was their meaning and belief about the Happy Hunting Grounds, or the Great Spirit.

Under the ancient custom practiced by the Sioux Indians and some other tribes, the child was named after something the Great Spirit had created, like the birds, the sky, mountains, the moon, the sun, stars, or clouds. He was not named by his parents, but by the medicine man and his mother's mother. If the grandmother was dead, the oldest woman relative took her place. The naming did not take place until fifty moons, or four years, had passed. When the day came he fasted for twenty-four hours and was then placed in a sweat house and into a pool of water called the "tears of the Great Spirit." At sunset, as the ceremony was being performed, the parents gazed into the east, and the child was told which tribe he belonged to and given the name which had been decided upon long before.

I was the first grandchild in my family. I can remember the ceremony when I was named. They called me To-Ka-Lu-Lu-Ta, meaning Red Fox. When I went to Carlisle Indian School, they enrolled me as William Red Fox. I have never used this English name, but have kept the one my grandmother and the medicine man gave me in 1874.

The expression "war paint" is frequently used to describe women who have colored their lips and cheeks and darkened their eyebrows. This has come down from the Indians, who have been shown in moving pictures with painted faces, especially in battle scenes. Many students have asked me why the Indians do that. It is true that some tribes daubed their faces with red dye before taking up arms against an enemy, but many did not. They used paint or dye for many different purposes. To most of them, colors had symbolic meaning. They signified happiness, sorrow, what tribe they belonged to, where they lived. White meant snow; yellow meant the moon; orange, the sun; green, the earth; light blue, heaven; dark blue, the beginning of day; and pink, the birth of a child.

Three red dots under the left eye and a line from the right eye to the jaw signified that the person lived by a body of water; a V shape on the forehead meant he lived in the mountains; a crowfoot on the temples meant a forest; and red lines from the eyes to the lobes of the ears with three short lines on the chin meant war.

When a woman painted her forehead and braided her hair she was signaling that she was married.

Many tribes expressed their beliefs, customs, and folklore by weaving different colors in blankets, rugs, baskets, and paintings on their pottery.

"What is an Indian marriage like?"

[1 6 7]

This is a question I am often asked in schools. The question might be, "How much does an Indian pay for a wife?"

I begin my answer and explanation by pointing out that marriage to the Indian is much more binding than it is to the Whites or Negroes or any European race. When a man and woman of these civilized "tribes" make a marriage before God in their churches, or before a judge or justice of peace, they can disregard it without difficulty if they don't want to live together. The same judge who had the power to bind them as man and wife can separate them by divorce. Often this happens, bringing hardship upon children.

Under the old tribal Indian laws, marriage was binding until death. The wedding ceremonies differed, but they were of a serious nature, and the Great Spirit was implored to give a blessing to the pair. Among the Sioux, it was the custom for the couple's parents to exchange gifts of friendship. The boy was inducted into the girl's tribe, for women were considered more important than men in creating and rearing children, and the genealogy of tribes and clans was traced through them.

In the marriage ceremonial of the Sioux, the father of the boy would light a pipe, then point the stem to the heavens above, and the others would chant a hymn to the Great Spirit. He would then place the pipe to his heart, put the stem into the mouth of the girl's mother, then into the mouth of the father, and finally into hers. She would hold it for a moment, then point the stem toward heaven while she and the mother of the boy blew into the bowl, sending a wisp of smoke upward to please the Great Spirit.

The girl's father would then repeat the ceremony. When the girl's mother and the boy had blown the last wisp of smoke from the pipe, the boy and girl were man and wife. This was the tribal custom of the Sioux long before the White man came.

"Why did you bury your dead on poles above the ground?"

That was another often-asked question.

All Indians did not bury their dead in this manner. Some tribes placed the body in the limbs of a tree; others put it in a tomb made of stones. In the Northwest, some tribes placed the body in a dugout and cast it adrift.

The Sioux "buried" their dead on poles 6 feet above the ground. The poles were called Wa-Jo-La. The body was left there for two weeks. Every morning at sunrise and evening at sunset the Indians gathered to chant a prayer to the Creator. After the period of mourning, they made a vault of stone, or prepared a place on the ground for the body, with the feet always pointing west. Their last service was to cover the resting place with a mound of earth, and to chant another prayer in memory of the one who had passed to his happy hunting ground, as they gazed toward the rising place of the sun.

Another question sometimes asked was "Why do the Indians place the things that belonged to the dead in the grave with them. or burn them and place the ashes in the grave?"

It was because the Indians felt that personal possessions belonged to the one who had passed on, not to the ones who lived. They did not want sisters and brothers fighting over them.

I have been asked why the Indian held the sun in reverence when he prayed.

The answer is that the sun was the smile of the Great Spirit. Without that smile, the Indian knew no one could exist upon this earth. The sun is the light and power of all things that have been created.

There were a few times when I encountered ridicule in my association with people who seemed to think that the Indian was a freak, especially if he happened to be in a luxury hotel and dressed in buckskin trousers and a vest decorated with elk's teeth and porcupine quills. That happend to me on March 15, 1913, when I was in Washington, D.C., for a conference with President Wilson.

Chief Hollow Horn Bear died while I was there. I was in the lobby of the National Hotel when a young woman came up to me and said:

"Can you speak English?" I told her that I could. She smiled and said:

"I'm from the sun."

"How did you get there?" I asked without changing expression.

"You misunderstand me," she explained. "I am from the Baltimore *Sun,* a morning newspaper."

"What can I do for you?" I asked.

"I want to know if Chief Hollow Horn Bear will wear his feathers, ride his pony, and eat his corn in the happy hunting ground."

I told her to get her paper and pencil ready and I would give her a story. When she was ready, I dictated this:

"The old chief will wear his feathers, ride his pony and eat his corn when you smell the flowers that they put on your grave. Put that in your Baltimore *Sun* morning newspaper."

More than once I was asked if it was true that Indian women did most of the work and that the men were lazy.

The Indian woman, or squaw, as the White man called her, did not perform all the hard work, as some people believe. Both the women and the men had their allotted tasks, and they never encroached on one another except in emergencies. The man hunted and fished for a living and fought to protect his family and the hunting ground of his tribe. He made his weapons and his canoe, and did many other tasks that were important for the welfare of the tribe. The woman cared for the children, tanned the hides, made clothing, and did other household duties. The women

[1 7 1]

of many tribes, including the Sioux, took down and put up the lodges or tepees when the people moved. They carried the burdens or placed them on the backs of horses or behind them on poles or drags when they traveled. It was necessary that they perform these duties in order to allow the men to protect the travelers from enemies and to scout out a route and secure food and other supplies that were needed. They tended their flocks of sheep and goats, cut down trees, hewed timber, cleared land and planted corn, and gathered buffalo chips for their fires. They also spent time with their children, and looked after them while the mother attended to other family duties. Many of the men made the beadwork and the feather decorations for their clothing and moccasins. As a rule, the division of duties between men and women was equal, and there was between them a spirit of cooperation that expressed itself in times of need.

I always smile when I hear people speak about the laziness of the Indian man and the slavelike existence of the Indian woman. As a matter of fact, many White women do more hard work than their husbands. They work in stores and offices all day and then go home and work for several more hours taking care of their homes and their children. The city man who works in an office or factory may stop on the way home for a beer, hoping his wife will have dinner prepared when he gets there. After eating, he turns on the television or looks at the newspaper while his wife cleans the dishes, puts the children to bed and then mends their clothes, or does the washing. This may be slightly overdrawn, but it at least illustrates my point that no matter what race we belong to, we have duties and responsibilities.

"Why were Indians so savage?"

This question is seldom asked directly, but it bobs to the surface in a roundabout way during discussions following lectures to schoolchildren, who often obtain their opinions from textbooks.

One of the accusations brought against the Indians is that they tortured their war prisoners. This practice, in fact, was universal among the tribes. It was so widely practiced and accepted that the average warrior felt dishonored if he was not tortured if made a prisoner by his enemies. It must also be remembered that the Indians, through their rugged environment and the self-discipline and denials it imposed, were able to withstand severe punishment without fear or cowardice. Neither must it be forgotten that the standards by which we judge cruelty and other matters are not the same among all races. What appears to one as extreme may be viewed by another as a natural expression of the environmental influences and racial characteristics.

No one ever saw an Indian wantonly destroy things that the Great Creator gave to man for his needs—the birds of the air, the fish, the wild game, the crystal-clear rivers and lakes, or the forests, swamps, and plains that gave him shelter. The Indian never shot a buffalo just to see how good a marksman he was, or to glory in the death of the animal, nor did he ever bend his bow and fire an arrow into the heart of a fawn. He fished and hunted only for his needs, and was careful not to destroy the animals and birds that supported him. When he caught a fish that was too small for his use, he threw it back into the water, not because he was more compassionate than the White man, but because he was a true conservationist. The Indian protected birds while they were nesting; the White man allows his cat to invade the nests and eat the young.

When I hear the word "savage" applied to the Indian, I am bewildered by the behavior of people who call themselves civilized and Christian. Do they live up to their religious teaching or the commandments? Did the Pilgrims and the English at Jamestown observe, or even think about those divine laws?

This discussion should have started with Columbus and his men when they first reached these shores. The Indians greeted them with friendship, provided them with fresh food, showered them with gifts, and in return, the captain and crew of the *Santa Maria* kidnapped several of the men, women, and children and took them back to Spain, where they were publicly exhibited as wild beasts.

That was the first act of barbarity against the native Americans, and as time passed and Columbus and other sea captains and admirals came, they took possession of the homes and land of the people, degraded them with whiskey, raped their wives and daughters, and introduced venereal diseases among them.

Some misinformed writers have reported that Columbus and his sailors contracted gonorrhea on their trips to America, but this and other genetic diseases were prevalent in Europe for centuries and in Egypt before the time of Christ. They were unknown among the Indians, and so were cancer, glaucoma, and many other diseases that afflicted people of the Old World.

In the early times, it was not uncommon for the Spaniards to butcher an Indian as they would a wild beast, to lend spice to a holiday celebration. On several occasions, Columbus called the Indians to festivities on Santo Domingo, then turned loose on them a pack of giant, savage hounds, while his men watched and applauded as the dogs fell upon shrieking, terrified Indian children, women, and men, tearing them to pieces and glutting themselves. The dons looked upon this sport as people do on a bullfight today. Within a few years after Columbus landed on Santo Domingo, all the Indians there were killed, deported, or enslaved.

Everywhere the Spanish sailors and adventurers went in the New World during those years of barbarism, they treated the natives as wild beasts. They looted the temples of the Aztec, Inca, and Mayan Indians, destroyed their cultures, and left a trail of blood and an imprint of suffering in their lands.

Merely to mention that the Spaniards of that age were treacherous and unjust would be to gloss over a piling-up of inhuman acts that brings tears to the eyes and regrets to the heart of anyone with understanding or compassion.

"Why do so many Indians return to their reservation after attending school?"

The question was asked more often in the past than it is today, for in early years when reservations and schools were first established the Indians were wards of the government and the students had to return. Many of them resented that, for they had crossed the bridge from their ancient civilization to the glamorous culture of the White man. A few were employed by the Indian Bureau as teachers, clerks, interpreters, nurses, and in other capacities.

Even after the restrictions were lifted and the Indians began to get citizenship rights, they found it difficult to obtain employment because of the widespread prejudice against them.

If an employer was thinking of hiring one, very likely he would be warned by a friend: "Say, John, you don't intend to hire that Redskin, do you? They are not worth a damn. They will steal anything you have."

That attitude held the Indians back for many years, while most of the students returned to their reservations where they could live without the distrust and suspicion they met everywhere on the outside.

Changes in the White man's point of view came gradually as men like Will Rogers, Vice-President Curtis, and the great athlete James Thorpe, who were part Indian, rose to places of prominence in the nation; and writers like Mary Austin and research by the Smithsonian Institution and several universities debunked the myths and misinformation about the Indians and brought them into proper perspective with accurate writing and reporting.

CHAPTER XVI

THE SHADOW OF OBLIVION

THE Bureau of Indian Affairs was established by Congress after most of the Indians had been captured and placed upon reservations. The cavalry had assassinated their leaders and their tribes were broken up and demoralized. In all this time only one Indian has been selected to head the bureau. That was Robert Benson, who was appointed by President Johnson in 1966. He was an Oneida from Wisconsin, a career man in the bureau. From his position at the top, where complete information was accessible, he became dismayed at the government's neglect of its Indian wards who were scattered on 241 reservations across the country. His attempts to bring about reforms and improvements through Congress and other sources failed. Everywhere he encountered apathy from officials who were occupied with what they considered more pressing problems. Frustrated and discouraged, he resigned in July, 1969, stating that the administration was "completely ignoring the Indian."

About that same time Senator Edward Kennedy, chairman of the subcommittee on Indian education, said:

"Our nation's policies and programs for educating American Indians are a national tragedy."

Another senator, Walter Mondale of Minnesota, added to this by charging that the Indian schools contain the elements of disaster. "The first thing an Indian learns is that he is a loser," he declared.

Speaking in similar vein McGeorge Bundy, President of the Ford Foundation, said:

"The American Indians are by any measure, save cultural heritage, the country's most disadvantaged minority."

A few Indians who occupy places of influence in White society have added bits of criticism to fill in the picture of neglect. Among them is Vine Deloria, a Standing Rock Sioux who, in the recent book *Our Brother's Keeper,* says:

"The Indians in White America angrily indict Whites for keeping the Indian a stranger in his homeland."

The extent of the suffering and deprivation among Indians is reflected by statistics obtained from the government in 1969, which showed that their life expectancy is forty-four years compared to seventy-one for the rest of the nation's population. Their average family income is $1,500. The average schooling for an Indian child is five and a half years, which is far below that for both Black and Mexican-American children. Statistics from another bureau in Washington are equally revealing and tragic. The suicide rate among Indian teen-agers is three times the national average, and on some reservations, it is ten times as high.

The facts that underlie these statistics are clearly defined in the neglect, poverty, and hopelessness that prevail almost everywhere on the reservations. Much of the land held in trust for the Indians by the government is unproductive. The Apache reservation in Arizona is an example. That is a picture-post-card region with skyscraping mountains covered with ponderosa, valleys of unforgettable loveliness, and inhospitable deserts; but it is unsuitable for farming, and many of the Indians live there in windowless wooden shacks with corrugated metal roofs and subsist on meager supplies from the scrawny hand of welfare, and the crops grow sparsely on a sprinkling of tillable soil. The sight of an Indian woman toting pails of water, a mile or more from her shack, is common, and the cesspool prevails as a symbol of status for the inhabitants.

America's preoccupation with the world wars, a shattering depression, and a multitude of other ethnic, social, and economic problems has left little time in the twentieth century for the nation to consider how the Indians were faring. They have been a neglected, almost forgotten minority, while most Americans believe they are being fed, clothed, sheltered and, in general, coddled by a benevolent government. They number only one-four-hundredth of the population. The Negroes are ten times as numerous, and much more vocal in making their needs and wants known. These two races differ in their backgrounds, ethnic traits, and aptitudes. While the Negro has become forceful in a competitive society, with oratory on his lips and a longing in his heart for equality, the Indian, developed through centuries by the adamant forces of nature, is a subdued, stoical figure.

In recent years, a faction has come to the front among Negroes urging them to maintain and perpetuate their racial and cultural identity. The leaders of this movement feel that the White man has left a vacuum that can be filled only by establishing man's identity with himself and nature. They assert that the Negro is a distinct unit in the spectrum of races and should be proud of his inheritance and achievements. This has always been fundamental in the composition of the Indian. He never bowed or fawned before the White man, or conceded superiority to his artificial culture. His faith in the Great Spirit sustained his faith in himself as an individual and welded his character to the ethical structure of morality and integrity.

There is not much intercourse between reservation Indians and the better class of White people. Race prejudice is the primary cause. There has been a trifling improvement in this attitude in recent years, but many Indians cling to their ancient customs and beliefs and this continues to set them apart from other races. Even the missionaries and teachers have been unable to convince them that White civilization is an improvement over the one developed by their ancestors. Business transactions are the main contacts between the two races. The Indians have separate churches and schools, separate fairs, dances, and community centers. Some of their children attend public schools, but even there prejudice exists, although not among officials and teachers. You can imagine a timid Indian boy of five or six years of age being greeted when he enters a public school by:

"Hi, Tonto, where's your horse?" or "Why didn't you bring your tomahawk?" Being sensitive, as all Indian children are, especially in the presence of Whites, the boy does not know how to respond and slinks into the school house, spiritually and mentally injured. There may have been no intention to ridicule him, but children are universally cruel without knowing it, and sensing that the boy is vulnerable, they continue to taunt him. An Indian boy or girl is a racial outcast in almost any elementary school among a White majority. The prejudice is inborn, and only the most perceptive teachers can eradicate it. In high school, if the Indian child gets that far, he has a better chance, for students of that age are more discerning and the virtue of compassion has developed, as a desert flower, at least in some of them.

The right to vote has not been of much benefit to the Indians. Every two years, during the heat of campaigns, both political parties manifest solicitude for them, but this disappears after the elections. The black-robed figure of injustice and the concealed hand of cruelty appeared in 1969 among the Navajos, who were reported to have been "reduced to Biafra-level malnutrition by greedy White traders and water-sponging farmers." Documented information on this was submitted to the United States Senate, and a member of that august body was shown in newspaper stories as a champion of the exploiters.

Time and again, the water resources of the Indians have been diverted to irrigate other lands, and countless acres have been confiscated for dams and public recreation parks. An example of this occurred in the 1950s when the Tuscaroras of New York had to relinquish 553 fertile acres for a reservoir. They were paid $850,000, but the Niagara University received $5,000,000 for 200 acres in the same vicinity. In 1924 the Army Corps of Engineers sliced off 10,000 acres from the Seneca Reservation for the Kinzua Dam, paying them $3,000,000 and engendering a lot of bitterness in the tribe.

The injustice that appears on the national scene

shows up in minor happenings on the reservation. The inner reactions of the Indians can well be imagined when they are present at scenes like that which I witnessed in the federal court at Deadwood, South Dakota:

An Indian youth was arrested and taken before the judge for illegal possession of liquor, and he was given a jail sentence. The Indians knew that the complaining official, the executive on the reservation, had plenty of liquor in his home and his "whiskey breath" could be detected while he testified; yet he was allowed to leave the courtroom (a hallowed place, the White man told them) with an air of satisfaction in knowing that his records would show another conviction of an Indian lawbreaker. That is an example of why the Indians do not cooperate wholeheartedly with the law enforcement officers. If given the responsibility of policing themselves on their reservations, they would be on the alert to prevent and detect crime, and to create the spirit of obedience to the laws. The young people would obey their officers, and the hostility they feel toward those whom they look upon as oppressors and enemies would cease to exist.

In the spring of 1969 the Associated Press published an article about a White trader, acting as postmaster, who plucked an old woman's welfare check as it went through the mail. The story continued:

"He barged into her hogan and demanded that she endorse the check. When she refused to sign it, he brandished a knife at her. Still she resisted, and he grabbed her hand, forced her thumb on an ink pad, and then forcibly 'endorsed' the check with her thumb-print. Two outraged property crop lawyers went to the trader and threatened him with charges of assault and battery and illegal conversion. The bully returned the check and settled the assault case with an additional $100."

Americans who run away to recreation parks and seashores on weekends and vacations no doubt have a nostalgia for the wilderness, an unconscious yearning for the rugged, the cruel, the gentle, and sometimes for solitary communion with the Great Spirit; but almost everywhere they go, they leave the campsites and beaches littered with the wrappings of civilization. They find a land despoiled by bulldozers and dredges that have torn down mountains, dammed rivers, and converted the beauty spots of nature into homesites to accommodate a population that is running wild. This is called "progress," a word that should be scissored from the dictionary and replaced by "predaceous."

Most of the Indians on reservations cling to their ancient ways, but through the years, many, discomfited by government restrictions and resigned to the passing of primitive America, have moved into White society and intermarried, and their blood runs through the biological potpourri that makes the nation a composite of all the races of mankind. Some have succeeded in professions and trades, but the majority have assembled in colonies, where they live in depression and squalor. Almost 60,000 are in Los Angeles, 20,000 in San Francisco, 15,000 in Chicago's North Side. Others are congregated in timeworn apartments and shabby dwellings in Phoenix, Minneapolis, and other cities.

There are some who recoil from the crammed-in slovenliness of urban life and return to the reservations, but more are overpowered by loneliness. Nature is a worshipful reality, and they cling to its frazzled edges with enduring respect and withered hopes.

A few activists implore them to ignore demands of the past and countenance the commanding culture of the White man, but the call of the wild does not die easily in the deep rivers of biology.

I have talked to some who gave up life in the cities and returned to their families and relatives. They found the city a smothering place of smoke, factory fumes, and canned foods, and beer parlors the only place where they could find companionship.

"The land and open spaces called me back," one young man said. "I would rather sit on a river bank and mourn for the past than accept what the White man has offered me."

One of the major problems of the Indians almost everywhere is alcohol. Before the White man introduced whiskey among them, they had never tasted strong drink, but the phrase "like a drunken Indian" came into the language in the seventeenth century. The trader found that a few drinks of whiskey conditioned the Indian for selling his furs, or even his homestead, for a pittance. Even the missionaries had little success in stopping that kind of thievery. The liquor problem, however, did not become endemic until the present century. Faced with an alien, hostile civilization, treated with contempt, and beaten down by despair, the Indian turned to drink as a means of escape. On one Western reservation 44 percent of the men and 21 percent of the women were arrested in one year for drunkenness. A statement by Bill Pensioneau, President of the National Indian Youth Council, amplified this:

"The only time we are free is when we are drunk."

White people who are unacquainted with the Indians and wish to visit their reservations should take warning to never judge the Indian's intelligence by his general appearance or actions, since in the presence of strangers he may sit on his horse and gaze out into space as though he had no interest in life, yet in reality, he has studied the White man and perhaps has a rather accurate picture of his station in life and his personality. His keen eye and silent tongue enable him to quickly comprehend new surroundings, a gift that has made him an excellent hunter and a great soldier.

Then too, the Indian horseman may be thinking

of how he has been regarded as a savage for decades because that was the only way the White man could justify his acts as he swept across America shooting everything in his gunsights.

CHAPTER XVII

PRAYER

O GREAT SPIRIT:

Forgive me for intruding into your domain. I should not try with my limited intelligence to grapple with the enigma of life, but I have been alive for one hundred years and witnessed the White man's conquest of a new continent that was as remote as Atlantis in the spring of 1492. That was when he used the wind to propel his boat across the water and either walked or rode a horse upon the land. It was before he had been entrusted with a telescope or enlightened about the law of gravity and the mysteries of the atom.

What I wonder in my intrusion is whether he has used your gifts with wisdom, or merely as contrivances to achieve what he calls "progress."

If happiness is the only good, he has not found it in the possession of new conveniences or luxuries. He was closer to contentment on horseback in the wilderness than he is on a jet plane in the skies. He has conquered the world, but not himself.

This new continent you showed him from what was left of your creation is now despoiled by his avaricious nature. He has dug the gold and silver from your hills, cut down the forests that processed the oxygen he breathed, and populated the land with people who live in a complex of impending disaster.

The clean streams have become open sewers to carry his refuse out to sea, and marine life perishes in the estuarian kindergartens from pesticides. He is facing a spring that will be silent, for birds are passing away in the poisonous environment that has replaced the primitive wilderness. They drift into shore on waves, embalmed in oil, or their eggs are infertile from the chemicals of death that pollute the land, air, and water.

There is a pessimism in truth and terror in prophecy. Perhaps what we see happening in your world, O Great Spirit, is a design—a final plague foreshadowing the destiny of man; or I may be thinking with embittered thoughts, a man who is no longer young in such a thoroughly finished world.

If our society is death-orientated, as Szent-Györgyi, the Nobel Prize–winning scientist believes, the conclusion of man's life on earth is inevitable; but I cling tenaciously to the hope that he has the perception and will power to overcome the evils he has fostered. He has the skill to remake the world if he possesses the desire; and it may be that youth, which is in revolt against the establishment, will quit floundering in futile exhibitionism and direct its energies to objectives that are imperative in the struggle for survival.

O Great Spirit, instruct the children of the White man in the wisdom of the past and the futility of the hours when they become lost in the wilderness of frustration. Counsel them to venerate truth and its companion virtues. Teach them to appreciate the simplicity and wonders of Nature, and to protect its wildlife against insensate tyrannies; and as they grow to maturity, let them learn the shattering uselessness of the conflicts and wars that indict their ancestors. Give them the formulas for freeing the air, water, and land of the poisons that have traumatized their environment.

From your creative hands, you gave my people a Garden of Eden between two oceans. They worshiped you with their eyes, their ears, and their thoughts. The flower and blade of grass spoke to them, and your songs were heard on the violin strings of the wind in the trees.

The Indian people you put here weep for what has happened. They have a sturdy background of morality and discipline. Forgive those who tried to remake them into the image of the White man, and let the wealth of their heritage be preserved as a vital force in the world, and not entombed in museums or consigned to oblivion.

This is my prayer!

Appendix:
From the Notebooks of
Chief Red Fox

*The following extracts are from the fourteen hand-written notebooks filled by Chief Red Fox. It was these notebooks that served as the source material for his memoirs.—*Ed.

THE BLACK HILL AS IT
WAS TOLD BY MY MOTHER

My mother told many times about my grandfather and the stories he told about the holy land of the Sioux.

Our holy land is known to my people as Paka-Sapa meaning Black Hills.

She told me how many tribes came from long distance to cure their sick and heal their wounds in the hot springs of sulphur and other mineral waters for winter camping and hunting. My grandfather believed that the dark of night turns the rocks into spirits and the strange chants awakening the echoes.

From the holes in the rock walls where the healing waters flow and the Indians fill their buffalo horn cups with the tears of the Great Spirit, meaning clear water, and drink it to cure.

From the highest rocks that touch the sky my grandfather calls the mighty spirit for his people.

The great deposits of glistening metals should be used for holy worship and never sold.

My grandfather knew of the gold there for many moons long before it was discovered by the White men in the year 1870.

Painting on rock walls made long before the coming of my people. They were read by our holy men as a guide on how to live, a teaching from the Great Creator.

The crystal caves hidden beneath the ground have great mystery.

It was on Bear Butte, Mato-Paka, that the father of my mother and my Uncle Crazy Horse performed the rites of a holy man and was given great power from The Great Creator who appeared to him in the form of a bear.

A great council was held at this Butte, where Chiefs talked over about giving the Black Hills over to The United States government.

There were many peaks in the Black Hills never climbed by the old time Indians because there was a strong belief that it was visited by the Thunder Bird.

Legend further adds that whenever the Thunder Bird stopped it caused much lightning and thunder in the Black Hills.

My mother tells this story about my grandfather as he had told it to her when she was a child.

Many years ago many Sioux Indians went into the Black Hills to gather lodge poles for their tepees and wild fruits.

They camped at foot of a hill. While the other Indians were sleeping he walked away and climbed to the top of this hill.

He raised his hands to the heavens above and prayed to the Mighty Spirit to watch over his children and their children to give them power, strength and good health to guide in peace or war.

"I am in my declining years, so I chose to give my great spiritual gift to my son, Crazy Horse, who is young and strong."

"He will use the gift of the Mighty Spirit to be a great leader of the Sioux."

The spiritual power that was given Crazy Horse as a sacred obligation at Bear Butte is believed by the Sioux to have helped to bring about the complete destruction of the troops of Custer on the 25th of June 1876.

The Great Spirit had given Crazy Horse an answer to my grandfather's prayer.

MY LIFE AS I LIVED IT

Born in a tepee on the Eleventh day of June 1870.

At Thunder Butte Dakota Territory.

Son of New-Evaw, meaning White Swan and Evan-ble-Spa, meaning Black Eagle in the Sioux Indian language.

They named me To-Ka-Lu-Lu-Ta, meaning Red Fox. At the government Indian school they gave me the name William.

In 1904 I was elected as the fifth-district council Chief. Now I am known as Chief William Red Fox my family name.

My mother is the sister of Chief Crazy Horse.

As a child I lived on the Pine Ridge Reservation Dakota Territory.

At the time of the Custer fight I was six years and fourteen days old.

I still remember that long hot and dusty journey from Pine Ridge to the Little Big Horn country in the state of Montana.

The day after the Custer fight, my mother and father and many other Indians who took part in that battle retreated into Canada.

*   *   *

My grandparents, sister, brother and myself with many old women, men, and children were returned back to the Pine Ridge and Standing Rock Reservation. Once the Reservation was called Woman Rock, named after a rock that looks like a woman.

General Alfred Terry was the commanding officer of the armed forces that returned us back home.

The day after that fight on 26th of June 1876 was the last time that I saw my mother and father until I returned back home from school in the month of May 1889.

At the age of seven they sent me in 1887 to the Fort Yates Indian school in the Standing Rock Reservation.

At the age of ten, they sent me to the Carlisle Indian school in the month of August 1880. The Carlisle School is in the City of Carlisle in the state of Pennsylvania.

This was new and strange life for me.

My first train ride, people would look at me as if I was a wild beast.

When I arrived at Carlisle they cut off my long hair and gave me new kind of clothes to wear and shoes that hurt my feet.

This new life was not like my life as an Indian.

I was sad and lonely, did not like the way that the White people lived.

There were many girls and boys from different tribes, many of them could speak in the Indian sign language. I could talk to them in sign language that my grandparents had taught me.

HOW INDIANS RECEIVED THEIR NAMES

You oftentimes have heard it said that an Indian received his name after the first thing his or her mother saw after the child is born or what the child dreams about or what he kills. All of this is hearsay not facts.

Nowadays some Indians believe that themselves.

I mean Indians living among the White people.

They don't know the real habits and customs of their own race.

You will find thousands of them.

They don't know anything about their own people's way of doing in real Indian way of life.

Some people will tell some of those Indians about the Indian dances or about the feathers they wear or painting their faces or their marriages or about their belief of the Happy Hunting Grounds.

When they are asked these things they will tell the people the things they read about in some book written by men who created such Ideas for his book. Many times such writers have never met an Indian or asked any about real Indian life or their customs.

THE NAMING OF A CHILD

In the early days the Indians had many customs they do not practice nowadays.

When a child is born the grandmother and the Medicine Man give the child his first tribal name.

The grandmother and Medicine Man are the only ones who then know this name.

If the grandmother is dead the oldest woman relation takes her place.

When a child is about fifty moons old that would be about four years old.

Then they named the child after what the Great Spirit had created or of the clan of his grandfather.

My family name is Red Fox. I did not adopt any English name like so many have. I keep the name my mother gave me in the year of 1874.

Many of the Indians have a tribal and also an English name that they adopted in the Army Navy Mission and Government Schools.

WAR PAINT

Many times people will say to an Indian where is your war paint.

It is true Indians of some tribes painted for war. Many tribes did not.

The paint was used for many different things.

It was used to show happiness, sorrow, peace, what tribe you belong to, where you lived, marriage. When the woman painted her forehead red and when she braided her hair the paint made her look like a half of a diamond, the symbol of marriage as other races wear a ring.

Many tribes expressed that by their paint.

They also express themselves to each other by the sign language by talking with their hands.

Many of these symbols were used in their bead work, blanket weaving, painting on their pottery, in the weaving of baskets.

Each color had a meaning. Their paint had many meanings, not just for war.

THIS IS THE CAUSE OF THE CUSTER FIGHT

Custer was very angry with President Grant and General Crook because he had some trouble with them several months before.

Now let's get the true facts about this: shortly before this campaign began, Custer had testified against Secretary of War William W. Belknap and had given testimony which implicated the President's brother, Orval Grant, in scandals of the Indian Bureau, although he had added nothing to what Orval Grant had previously admitted under oath.

*   *   *

President Grant removed Custer from his command and only the pleas of Brig. General Alfred H. Terry, Custer's immediate superior, saved him from the disgrace of his regiment marching without him. They say he was only sent there as a watchdog, no orders to fight the Indians.

Custer thought that a victory was the only way to get back his command.

*   *   *

From the time Custer left Fort Lincoln, the Indians knew where he was.

Indian scouts kept him in sight all the time.

Some young Indians, who left Wolf Point Reservation, left a trail that Custer was able to follow.

On June 23rd he was within twenty miles of our villages.

*   *   *

He camped for the night of June 24th within eight miles from where he met his defeat.

On June 25th, which was a Sunday, the Chaplain held his services and prayed for a victory, I was told by Captain Godfrey.

*   *   *

About 11 A.M. that morning many of the children were playing when one of the little girls pointed to the East and said, "Witchie," meaning White man coming.

*   *   *

Young Indians who were herding horses closely brought them in and the Chiefs and Warriors got ready for the attack.

The old women and children and old men were taken to safety. The Indians always look after the ones that they thought were in danger. We were well protected by three hundred young braves. I was six years and fourteen days old at that time.

[203]

* * *

Custer came to a halt about noon, then the Indians knew that he had divided his men into four different groups.

He told Major Reno to cross the river and make the attack from the West and Captain Benteen to attack from the North East.

He told McDugal and Captain Godfrey to bring up the pack train and wagons, and he would meet them on the west bank of the Rose Bud River.

He also told Major Reno, Captain A. A. Cook, and Captain Benteen he would make the attack about 4 P.M. and for them to rest their men and horses until then.

* * *

About 2 P.M. we heard shots fired at a distance.

Later it was known that my father, Black Eagle and Black Elk had blocked Benteen.

Crow Dogs and Two Strikes stopped Reno and drove him across the River.

*　　　*　　　*

Kicking Bear and Many Horses blocked McDugal and Godfrey with their pack train and wagons.

*　　　*　　　*

The other Warriors under Chief Gall, Chief Two Moons, and my uncle, Chief Crazy Horse, had mounted their horses and were ready for the attack.

*　　　*　　　*

Custer's scouts, Boyer and Curley the Crow Indian scout, told him not to head for the river.

He cursed them in reply, as I was told by Theodore Goldwin, who left Custer with a message for General Terry, also by John Martin the bugler, who went to General Gibron for reinforcements, and by Kanipe, who was left a few miles back from where the attack was made. He was caring for several sick soldiers.

*　　　*　　　*

They were the last three white men to see him alive. They never claimed to be in the fight.

[2 0 5]

Curley the Crow as he was known was the last of his command to see him alive and was the lone survivor of that fight.

Curley died at Hardin, Montana, in the year 1918, John Martin died at Norwalk, Ohio, in 1916, Theodore Goldwin died at the Masonic Home in Wisconsin, 1926, Kanipe died in Ashville, North Carolina, about 1948. He has a nephew, a barber, living in Corpus Christi, Texas, and several children and grandchildren living in North Carolina.

*   *   *

Someone said Rain-In-The-Face killed Custer. Someone wrote a story saying that White Bull killed Custer.

White Bull was eleven years old at that time.

Several years ago, someone wrote that One Bull told him thirty-five years ago that he killed Custer and the reason he did not tell his story before One Bull died was because One Bull thought that the government would punish him for the killing of Custer.

Now you must remember that One Bull could not speak English. He was with me on the Buffalo Bill Wild West Show when we went to Europe for two years and I never heard him claim the killing of Custer.

*   *   *

I believe what my mother and father and many of the old Indians have said.

No one knows who killed Custer or when he fell.

They all say the bullets came from the Indians' guns just like hail.

No Indian that I know of has claimed the honor of killing Custer.

General Hugh L. Scott has said that military records show that he had powder burns on his temple and he did not have long hair at the time of the fight.

You have read many stories about Custer's last fight, seen movies and TV shows about him. They make a great hero out of him and have him standing to the last.

The only thing that gave the TV and story writers and movie directors their ideas about Custer standing to the last man in that battle was a picture that someone painted in the year of 1877 for the Anheuser-Busch Brewery of Saint Louis, Missouri.

*   *   *

The artist created an idea about the battle of Little Big Horn or Custer's last fight.

There must be a character to outset this painting to attract the attention of the public.

The Idea of that artist gave writers and directors their idea that he was the last to die.

Chapter 2
This is the cause of the Custer fights

Custer was very angry with President Grant
and General Crook because he had some
trouble with them several month before.
Now let's get the true facts about this;
shortly before this campaign began, Custer
had testified against secretary of War
William W. Belknap and had given testimony
which implicated the President's brother,
Orval Grant in scandals of the Indian
Bureau,
Although he had added nothing to what
Orval Grant had previously admitted
under oath.

President Grant removed Custer from
his Comand, and only the pleas of
Brig. Gen. Alfred H. Terry, Custer immediate
superior had saved him from the
disgrace of his regiment marching
without him they say he was only
sent their as a watch dog no orders to
fight the Indians,
Custer thoughts that a victory was
his only way to get back his Command